Better Homes and Gardens®

ENCYCLOPEDIA
of
COOKING

Volume 13

Entice both family and guests with flavorful Veal Scallopine served over hot, buttered noodles. Garnish with a generous sprinkling of snipped parsley, if desired.

On the cover: Dinner by candlelight is an appropriate setting for Spanish Paella. This entrée offers an exotic blend of chicken, clams, rice, and vegetables accented with saffron.

BETTER HOMES AND GARDENS BOOKS
NEW YORK • DES MOINES

© Meredith Corporation, 1970, 1971, 1973. All Rights Reserved.
Printed in the United States of America.
Special Edition. First Printing.
Library of Congress Catalog Card Number: 73-83173
SBN: 696-02033-5

OSWEGO TEA *(o swē' gō)* — Another name for the herb red bergamot. It is used by the Oswego Indians for brewing tea.

OUNCE — A unit of weight equal to one-sixteenth of a pound. A fluid ounce, by volume, equals one-eighth of a cup.

OUTDOOR COOKERY — A method of preparing food over an open campfire or heated charcoal. (See *Barbecue, Campfire Cookery* for additional information.)

OUZO *(ōō' zō)* — The anise-flavored brandy that is the national aperitif of Greece. It is usually drunk as a mixture of four or five parts cold water to one part ouzo. When mixed with water, it turns white.

OVEN — An enclosed unit used for cooking food. Primitive ovens, fashioned from clay and heated with a wood fire, contrast greatly with today's ovens, which are heated with gas or electricity. The newest type of oven, the electronic unit, utilizes microwaves. (See *Electronic Cookery, Equipment* for additional information.)

Oven temperatures

Very slow oven	250° to 275°
Slow oven	300° to 325°
Moderate oven	350° to 375°
Hot oven	400° to 425°
Very hot oven	450° to 475°
Extremely hot oven	500° to 525°

OVEN-FRY — A method of cooking in which food is coated with seasoned flour or crumbs and baked in the oven so as to give it the flavor and appearance of pan-fried foods. For example, cut-up poultry is dredged in seasoned flour, rolled in melted butter, and placed in a single layer in a shallow pan before baking in a hot oven. Or thinly sliced potatoes or crumbed eggplant slices are dotted with butter and similarly baked. A very hot oven is used for crumb-dipped fish fillets.

Onion Fries

Dip 16 ounces frozen French-fried potatoes in ¼ cup melted butter. Place 1 envelope onion soup mix in clear plastic bag. Add potatoes, few at a time; shake till coated. Place potatoes in 13x9x2-inch baking pan. Bake at 425° for 20 minutes, turning once. Serves 6.

Chicken in Chips

Barbecued potato chips and Parmesan cheese add a special flavor to the crunchy coating—

 ½ cup evaporated milk
 2 tablespoons grated Parmesan cheese
 1 tablespoon lemon juice
 ¼ teaspoon paprika
   Dash pepper
    . . .
 1 2½- to 3-pound ready-to-cook broiler-fryer chicken, cut up
 1 5½-ounce package barbecued potato chips, coarsely crushed

In shallow bowl combine evaporated milk, Parmesan cheese, lemon juice, paprika, and pepper. Dip chicken pieces in milk mixture, then roll in coarsely crushed potato chips. Place chicken pieces, skin side up, in greased, shallow baking pan. Bake chicken at 375° till tender, about 1 hour. Do not turn. Makes 4 servings.

Tater-Coated Chicken

 1 slightly beaten egg
 2 tablespoons water
 ½ teaspoon seasoned salt
 1 2½- to 3-pound ready-to-cook broiler-fryer chicken, cut up
 1 cup packaged instant mashed potato flakes
   Salt
   Pepper
 ¼ cup butter or margarine

Mix egg, water, and seasoned salt. Dip chicken in the mixture; roll in potato flakes. Sprinkle with salt and pepper. Melt butter in shallow baking pan. Place chicken in pan, skin side up. Bake at 375° till done, about 1 hour. Serves 4.

Oven-Fried Frog Legs

Sample this delicacy at home—

>   2 pounds fresh or frozen frog legs
> 1/4 cup butter or margarine,
>   melted
> 2/3 cup fine saltine cracker crumbs
>
>   • • •
>
>   6 lemon wedges
>   (optional)

Thaw frozen frog legs. Secure frog legs at joints with string. Brush with melted butter or margarine; then roll in cracker crumbs.* Place frog legs in single layer on well-greased shallow baking pan. Bake at 375° till done, about 1 hour. Do not turn during cooking. Remove strings from frog legs and serve with lemon wedges, if desired. Makes 6 servings.

*Or substitute one envelope seasoned coating mix for the cracker crumbs and omit the butter. Use mix according to package directions.

Oven Chicken Fricassee

Serve this dish with rice as an accompaniment, a green vegetable, and gelatin salad—

>   3 tablespoons all-purpose flour
>   1 teaspoon salt
>   1 teaspoon paprika
>
>   • • •
>
>   1 2 1/2- to 3-pound ready-to-cook
>   broiler-fryer chicken, cut up
>   2 tablespoons butter or margarine,
>   melted
>   1 10 1/2-ounce can condensed cream
>   of mushroom soup
> 2/3 cup evaporated milk

Combine flour, salt, and paprika. Brush chicken with melted butter or margarine; coat with flour mixture. Arrange chicken in an 11¾x7½x 1¾-inch baking dish. Bake at 375° for 20 minutes. Drain off excess fat.

Meanwhile, in small saucepan combine cream of mushroom soup and evaporated milk; cook and stir till heated through. Pour soup mixture over chicken. Cover baking dish with foil. Continue baking till chicken is tender, about 40 minutes longer. Remove foil the last 10 minutes. Makes 4 servings.

Sesame Chicken

Carry the cold chicken to a picnic in an ice chest or insulated container to keep it well chilled—

>   1 cup finely crushed saltine crackers
>   (about 27)
> 1/3 cup sesame seed, toasted
>   1 teaspoon paprika
> 1/2 teaspoon salt
>
>   • • •
>
> 20 chicken drumsticks
> 1/3 cup evaporated milk
> 3/4 cup butter or margarine, melted

Combine cracker crumbs, toasted sesame seeds, paprika, and salt. Dip chicken drumsticks in evaporated milk; roll in crumb mixture. Pour melted butter or margarine into 13½x8¾x1¾-inch baking dish or a jelly roll pan. Place chicken drumsticks in pan; turn once. Bake at 375° for 70 minutes. Remove chicken from pan. Cover; chill. Makes 10 servings.

Oven Tomato Sandwich

Oven-fry the bacon to save watching and turning—

>   8 slices bacon, cut in half
>   Butter or margarine,
>   softened
>   4 slices French bread, cut 1 inch
>   thick
>   4 thick slices tomato
>
>   • • •
>
> 1/2 cup mayonnaise or salad dressing
> 1/3 cup grated Parmesan cheese
>   2 tablespoons milk
>   1 tablespoon instant minced onion
>   1 teaspoon Worcestershire sauce

Preheat oven to 400.° Put separated bacon slices on a rack in shallow baking pan. Bake at 400° for 10 minutes. Meanwhile, butter French bread. Put bread slices on baking sheet and toast on one side in oven, about 5 minutes. Remove bread from oven and turn; place tomato slices on untoasted sides. Combine mayonnaise or salad dressing, Parmesan cheese, milk, instant minced onion, and Worcestershire sauce. Spread over tomato slices. Bake sandwiches at 400° till golden, about 5 minutes. Top with cooked bacon slices. Makes 4 servings.

Easy Onion Chicken

    1 envelope onion salad dressing
       mix
   ½ cup butter or margarine,
       softened
    1 teaspoon paprika
    1 2½- to 3-pound ready-to-cook
       broiler-fryer chicken, cut up
   ¾ cup fine dry bread crumbs
      Paprika

Combine salad dressing mix, softened butter or margarine, and 1 teaspoon paprika. Spread butter mixture over chicken pieces. Roll pieces in fine dry bread crumbs to coat. Sprinkle with additional paprika for added color. Place chicken pieces in greased, shallow baking pan, skin side up. Bake at 375° till tender, about 1 hour; do not turn. Serves 4.

Oven Turkey Croquettes

    2 tablespoons butter or margarine
    3 tablespoons all-purpose flour
   ½ cup milk
   ½ cup chicken broth
    2 cups diced, cooked turkey
    1 tablespoon snipped parsley
   ¼ teaspoon dried rosemary leaves,
       crushed
      Salt
    6 to 8 slices bread
    1 beaten egg
      Melted butter or margarine
    1 cup canned jellied cranberry
       sauce
   ¼ cup claret

In saucepan melt 2 tablespoons butter; blend in flour. Add milk and chicken broth. Cook and stir till thickened and bubbly; cool. Stir in turkey, parsley, and rosemary; salt to taste. Cover; chill several hours.

Trim crusts from bread; tear bread slices into ½-inch pieces. Shape turkey mixture into 8 balls, using ¼ cup mixture for each.

Dip balls into egg, then roll in bread pieces, coating well. Place in greased, shallow baking pan. Brush with melted butter. Bake at 350° till hot and toasted, about 25 minutes. Meanwhile, heat cranberry sauce with claret; beat till smooth. Serve with turkey balls. Serves 4.

OX JOINTS, OXTAIL—The tail of the beef animal cut crosswise into 1½- to 2-inch pieces. Ox joints don't have much meat on them, yet they are very flavorful when braised with vegetables or used in stews.

Old-Time Oxtail Stew

Savor the rich and wonderful aroma of this tempting, main-dish stew while it cooks—

    2 pounds oxtail, cut in 1½-inch
       lengths
      All-purpose flour
    2 tablespoons shortening
      . . .
    1 medium onion, sliced
    1 16-ounce can tomatoes (2 cups)
    1 10½-ounce can condensed
       beef broth
  1½ teaspoons salt
   ¼ teaspoon pepper
      . . .
    8 small onions, halved
    4 potatoes, peeled and quartered
    4 carrots, peeled and quartered

Coat meat pieces with all-purpose flour. In Dutch oven brown meat on all sides in hot shortening. Add sliced onion, tomatoes, condensed beef broth, salt, and pepper. Cover; simmer meat mixture till meat is just tender, about 2 hours. Add halved onions, quartered potatoes, and quartered carrots; cover and simmer 1 hour longer. Skim off excess fat. Remove meat and vegetables to serving bowl.

To thicken meat broth, blend a little additional all-purpose flour with a small amount of cold water. (Amount of flour depends on amount of broth.) Stir into hot broth; cook and stir till thickened and bubbly. Cook and stir 1 to 2 minutes. Spoon over meat and vegetables.

For pressure pan: Coat meat with flour; brown on all sides in hot shortening. Add sliced onion, tomatoes, condensed beef broth, salt, and pepper. Cook at 15 pounds pressure for 35 minutes. Reduce pressure under cold running water. Add halved onions, potatoes, and carrots; return to 15 pounds pressure and cook for 10 minutes. Reduce pressure under cold running water. Skim off excess fat. Remove meat and vegetables to serving bowl. Thicken broth as above. Makes 6 servings.

OYSTER—A shellfish with a rough, oblong shaped shell, and a grayish white flesh. The oyster, in the same category with the clam, mussel, and scallop, has a soft body enclosed in a two-part shell. The bottom half of the shell is curved and holds the body while the top half is more flat-shaped. These two parts are held together at the hinge by an elastic ligament.

Any brief description of an oyster must cloud the warm respect true-oyster gourmets have for the oyster. Although this is a nutritious shellfish, the oyster has most often been used as an appetizer.

This was true of the ancient Greeks and the Romans who quaffed many oysters as a prelude to lavish banquets. So heavy was the demand for oysters during ancient times that after Julius Caesar overran Britain, he packed large quantities of the superb British oysters in snow and ice and shipped them off to Roman banquet halls.

The long-standing popularity of the oyster is probably due to its dual nature: When you open an oyster you either discover the delicious oyster meat or else (if you're lucky) a beautiful pearl.

Whatever the reason, the Europeans discovered mounds of oyster shells on the shores when they first landed on America.

How oysters are cultivated: Oyster beds, located on the bottoms of seas and bays, are cultivated to produce large numbers of good quality oysters. Fishermen who own or lease these beds from the government provide a good environment for the development of oysters.

The beds are cleared of any debris and animals that could attack the oyster before spawning season. After the baby oysters have hatched and have gone through a free-swimming stage, they are ready to sink to the bottom. Here, they cement themselves to a clean, hard surface, a process called "setting." Fishermen place

Christmas Eve dinner

← Ladle rich, buttery Oyster Stew from a tureen into warmed bowls for a traditional beginning of the holiday celebration.

shells, tiles, rocks or tree branches in the beds shortly before the setting, so there will be space for oysters to locate.

Once the "setting" has been accomplished, the oysters are transplanted to an area where they can grow faster. This step also serves to separate clusters of the animals, giving them more room to grow.

Finally the oysters are moved for the last time. This time to a fattening area. Once a desired size is achieved, the oysters are harvested with long-handled tongs and dredges towed behind boats. Then, they are taken to processing plants where some are graded and packed in the shell. Others are shucked (shells removed) and packed in small containers, frozen, or canned.

Because oysters which filter their food from the sea are often eaten raw, strict sanitary regulations are enforced in the oyster industry. In addition, to these regulations, health authorities supervise the cleanliness of the waters where the oysters grow, the places and equipment involved in the processing, and even the employees who work with the oysters.

Nutritional value: Oysters contain protein, calcium, phosphorus, iron, and B vitamins. They also contain copper which imparts a greenish color to the oysters. The calorie count for 5 to 8 raw, medium Eastern oysters is about 65; the calorie count for Pacific oysters, which are larger, is slightly higher. Frying or preparing the oysters in a rich sauce adds more calories.

Types of oysters: The principle types of oysters in America are the Eastern, Olympia, and Pacific. However, various types of oysters are found around the world in the shallow, brackish, or salt water of all coasts except those with polar waters.

The Eastern oyster, harvested from Massachusetts to Texas, comprises the majority of the domestic production. The small Olympia oyster, which is scarce, lives in the Pacific coastal waters from Washington to Mexico. The Pacific or Japanese oyster is also cultivated on the Pacific Coast. Transported from Japan in 1902, the Pacific or Japanese oyster is the largest of the three types, usually about as large as the palm of a person's hand.

Bluepoint, Lynnhaven, and Cape Cod oysters once meant those from a particular area. However, these terms now apply to types and can be from several areas. Chincoteague oysters are native to the Chesapeake Bay and Colchester oysters are a prized type of oyster from England.

Buying oysters: Allow approximately 6 oysters for an average serving, although more will be needed for avid oyster fans. The famous American gourmond, Diamond Jim Brady, often consumed 2 or 3 dozen oysters at the beginning of a meal. Few people however, have the capacity, in appetite or budget, to indulge so lavishly.

Oysters are available in the market as live in-the-shell, shucked, frozen, and canned. When buying those in the shell, be sure they are alive. The shell should close tightly when handled. These are usually sold by the dozen.

Shucked oysters are sold by the half-pint, pint, quart, and dozen. Select those that are plump and have a natural creamy color. The liquid should be clear and amount to only 10 percent of the total weight. Some markets will furnish shells with these for serving on the half shell.

Shucked oysters are also canned and frozen. These include ones frozen with a breading, and smoked oysters in cans.

Buy small oysters for eating raw or for use in cocktails. Medium ones are good for eating raw or cooking in stews and casseroles. The large sizes are best for frying. Grades are a guide to the sizes.

How to store oysters: Oysters may be stored longer than most shellfish. Those in the shell can be refrigerated for several days and shucked ones for 7 to 10 days.

Freezing oysters prolongs the storage time. Shuck and pack into freezer containers, leaving ½-inch headspace. These will keep 3 months. Thaw in the refrigerator while wrapped, and use immediately.

How to shuck: Wash and rinse each oyster in cold water. Hold the shell firm and insert a knife between the halves. (The knife is easier to insert if the thin end of the shell has been broken off with a hammer.) Cut around the opening and pry the shell open. Pull top half up and cut muscles free. Remove top half of shell if serving on the half shell. (See *Clam* for illustration of shucking.)

Check to see that all shell is removed, as small pieces often cling to the muscle.

Using a mechanical shucker speeds up the process or, if desired, fish markets will shuck oysters upon request.

How to cook oysters: Little, if any, cooking is needed for oysters. They are eaten chilled and raw with a dash of lemon juice, pepper, hot pepper sauce, or cocktail sauce and crackers or rye bread. Oysters are also cooked, but only for a few minutes. They are done when the edges curl, for too much cooking makes oysters tough.

Oysters are used in many different combinations. They can be used in baked, fried, stewed, scalloped, and creamed dishes. (See also *Shellfish.*)

Grades of oysters	
Eastern oysters	Oysters per gallon
Counts or Extra Large	160 or less
Extra Selects or Large	161 to 210
Selects or Medium	211 to 300
Standards or Small	301 to 500
Standards or Very Small	Over 500
Pacific oysters	
Large	64 or less
Medium	65 to 96
Small	97 to 144
Very Small	Over 144

Oysters on the Half Shell

Open small oysters. With knife, loosen each from shell, leaving in deep half of shell. Serve on bed of cracked ice with a commercially prepared or homemade cocktail sauce

Oyster Cocktail

Serve fresh shucked oysters, drained and chilled, in lettuce-lined cocktail cups. Spoon a cocktail sauce of your choice over oysters. One pint of oysters makes 6 servings.

Bring Scalloped Oysters to the table hot from the oven. This elegant main dish keeps the secret of how easy it is to prepare.

Oyster Pudding

Oysters and cheese make an unbeatable combination in this entrée for a late-night supper—

>   6 slices white bread
>   Butter or margarine, softened
>   6 slices sharp process American
>   cheese (6 ounces)
>   . . .
>   1 pint shucked fresh oysters
>   Milk
>   . . .
>   2 beaten eggs
>   1 teaspoon salt
>   1/4 teaspoon pepper

Spread bread slices lightly on one side with softened butter. Cut in cubes. Place *half* the cubes in bottom of an 11¾x7½x1¾-inch baking dish; top with sharp process cheese slices.

Drain oysters, reserving the liquid. Add enough milk to liquid to make 2½ cups. Arrange oysters on cheese. Top with remaining bread cubes. Combine milk mixture, eggs, salt, and pepper; pour over all in baking dish.

Bake pudding mixture at 325° till knife inserted just off-center comes out clean, about 1 to 1¼ hours. Makes 4 to 6 servings.

Scalloped Oysters

>   1 pint shucked fresh oysters
>   2 cups medium-coarse cracker
>   crumbs (46 crackers)
>   1/2 cup butter or margarine, melted
>   Pepper
>   . . .
>   3/4 cup light cream
>   1/4 teaspoon salt
>   1/4 teaspoon Worcestershire sauce

Drain oysters, reserving ¼ cup liquid. Combine cracker crumbs and butter. Spread a *third* of the crumb mixture in 8x1½-inch round pan. Cover with *half* of the oysters. Sprinkle with pepper. Using another *third* of the crumbs, sprinkle a second crumb layer over oysters; cover with remaining oysters. Sprinkle with pepper.

Combine light cream, reserved oyster liquid, salt, and Worcestershire sauce. Pour cream mixture over oyster and crumb layers. Sprinkle top with remaining crumbs. Bake at 350° till done, about 40 minutes. Makes 4 servings.

Corn-Oyster Scallop

Add a crisp salad and beverage for a supper menu

>   1 16-ounce can cream-style corn
>   1 10-ounce can frozen condensed
>   oyster stew, thawed
>   1 cup coarsely crushed crackers
>   (about 22 crackers)
>   1 cup milk
>   1 slightly beaten egg
>   1/4 cup finely chopped celery
>   1 tablespoon finely chopped canned
>   pimiento
>   1/4 teaspoon salt
>   Dash pepper
>   2 tablespoons butter or margarine,
>   melted
>   1/2 cup coarsely crushed crackers
>   (about 11 crackers)

Combine corn, oyster stew, the 1 cup cracker crumbs, milk, egg, celery, pimiento, salt, and pepper. Pour into greased 1½-quart casserole.

Combine melted butter or margarine and the ½ cup crumbs; sprinkle atop casserole mixture. Bake at 350° till knife inserted off-center comes out clean, about 1 hour. Makes 6 servings.

Deviled Oysters on the Half Shell

14 fresh oysters in shell
2 tablespoons finely chopped
   shallots
1 tablespoon butter or margarine
2 tablespoons all-purpose flour
½ teaspoon salt
⅛ teaspoon ground nutmeg
   Dash cayenne
1 tablespoon Worcestershire sauce
½ teaspoon chopped parsley
½ teaspoon prepared mustard
1 3-ounce can chopped mushrooms,
   drained

. . .

1 slightly beaten egg yolk
½ cup cracker crumbs
1 tablespoon butter or margarine,
   melted

Open oysters and reserve ⅓ cup of the liquid. With a knife, remove oysters from shells; wash thoroughly and chop. Wash shells. Cook shallots in 1 tablespoon butter till just tender; blend in flour and let brown. Stir in reserved oyster liquid, salt, nutmeg, cayenne, Worcestershire, parsley, mustard, and mushrooms; add oysters. Cook mixture about 3 minutes, stirring constantly. Remove from heat and stir in egg yolk. Spoon mixture into deep halves of oyster shells. Combine cracker crumbs and 1 tablespoon melted butter or margarine; sprinkle over oyster mixture. Bake at 350° for about 10 minutes. Serve immediately. Makes 2 or 3 servings.

Oyster Stuffing

Traditional holiday stuffing for turkey—

Cook ½ cup chopped celery, ½ cup chopped onion, and 1 bay leaf in ¼ cup butter till vegetables are tender; discard bay leaf. Add 6 cups dry bread cubes and 1 tablespoon snipped parsley to butter mixture; mix thoroughly.

Drain 1 pint fresh shucked oysters, reserving liquid; chop oysters. Add oysters, 2 beaten eggs, 1 teaspoon salt, 1 teaspoon poultry seasoning, and dash pepper to bread mixture; mix well. Add milk to reserved oyster liquid to make ¼ to ⅓ cup; add enough of the milk mixture to stuffing to moisten. Makes enough stuffing for one 10-pound turkey.

Oyster Stew

Pictured on page 1542—

2 tablespoons all-purpose flour
1½ teaspoons salt
1 teaspoon Worcestershire sauce
   Dash bottled hot pepper sauce
1 pint fresh shucked oysters,
   undrained
¼ cup butter or margarine
4 cups milk, scalded
   Butter
   Rich round crackers
   Canned pimiento cut into stars

Blend flour, salt, Worcestershire sauce, hot pepper sauce, and 2 tablespoons water in a 3-quart soup kettle. Add undrained oysters and the ¼ cup butter. Simmer over very low heat till edges of oysters curl, 3 to 4 minutes, stirring gently. Add hot milk; remove from heat and cover. Let stand 15 minutes. Reheat briefly. Pour into warm tureen or soup bowls. Top with pats of butter. Garnish by floating rich round crackers topped with pimiento stars atop stew. Makes 4 or 5 servings.

Hearty Oyster Stew

½ cup finely diced carrots
½ cup finely diced celery
½ cup butter or margarine
2 tablespoons all-purpose flour
1½ teaspoons salt
1 teaspoon Worcestershire sauce
   Dash bottled hot pepper sauce
2 10-ounce cans oysters (2¼ cups)
3 cups milk, scalded
1 cup light cream, scalded
   Paprika

In large saucepan cook carrots and celery in ¼ *cup of the butter* until tender. Add a smooth mixture of flour, salt, Worcestershire sauce, hot pepper sauce, and 2 tablespoons cold water. Add oysters with liquid. Return to boiling; simmer over very low heat 3 to 4 minutes, stirring gently. Add hot milk and cream. Remove from heat. Cover; let stand for 15 minutes.

Place remaining ¼ cup butter in tureen. Reheat stew to serving temperature. Pour into tureen; dash with paprika. Serves 4 to 6.

Deep-Fried Oysters

Be prepared to serve second helpings—

Drain fresh shucked oysters; dry between paper toweling. Roll each oyster in all-purpose flour seasoned with salt and pepper. Dip into mixture of 1 beaten egg and 1 tablespoon water, then dip in fine dry bread crumbs.

Fry till golden in deep hot fat (375°), about 2 minutes. Drain on paper toweling. Serve hot; pass commercially made tartar sauce or homemade sauce. (See *Tartar Sauce* for recipe.)

OYSTER CRAB—A tiny crab that lives inside the shell of an oyster. Oyster crabs are commonly called pea crabs. Their presence is often undetected due to their small size; consequently, they are sometimes unknowingly eaten along with the oysters when the oysters are served raw. Connoisseurs consider oyster crabs a great delicacy. These minute animals are especially prized for use in a succulent bisque.

OYSTER CRACKER, OYSTERETTE — A small, round, puffy cracker served with oysters. These crisp, salty crackers are also delicious eaten with soups, clams, salads, and assorted seafood cocktails.

OYSTER PLANT—Another name for the salsify plant. The edible roots have an oysterlike flavor. (See also *Salsify*.)

OYSTER SAUCE—A creamy sauce filled with chopped oysters that is served with poultry, such as turkey. In oriental cookery, an oyster sauce made by cooking oysters in soy sauce and brine is a popular dish.

OYSTERS ROCKEFELLER—A famous dish of oysters broiled or baked on the half shell. The original recipe was created by Antoine's, a famous New Orleans restaurant. This recipe included at least 18 ingredients, but the exact combination has always been a closely regarded secret. The dish was so rich that they named it after one of the country's wealthiest men.

Many variations of the original Oysters Rockefeller have been developed. Most contain a mixture of chopped spinach, butter, herbs, and bread crumbs, spread over the oysters on a half shell. (Spinach was not an ingredient in the original recipe.) The half shells are balanced on rock salt and then broiled or baked.

Oysters Rockefeller

   24 fresh oysters in shells
    2 tablespoons snipped parsley
    1 tablespoon chopped onion
    1 tablespoon butter, melted
      Salt
      Pepper
      Paprika
    1 cup cooked chopped spinach
  1/4 cup fine dry bread crumbs
  1/2 cup butter

Open oyster shells. With knife, remove oysters and drain. Wash shells; place each oyster in deep half of shell. Mix parsley, onion, and *1 tablespoon* butter; drizzle over oysters. Season with salt, pepper, and paprika to taste. Top *each* oyster with 2 teaspoons spinach, 1/2 teaspoon crumbs, and 1 teaspoon butter. Heat on bed of rock salt at 450° for 10 minutes. Makes 4 main-dish servings or 8 appetizer servings.

For a gourmet appetizer, arrange Oysters Rockefeller, baked either in oyster half shells or coquilles, on a bed of rock salt.

P

PAELLA (*pä ä′ luh, pä e′ yä*) — 1. A classic Spanish main dish usually consisting of rice, saffron, seafood, chicken, and vegetables cooked in olive oil. 2. The round Spanish baking pan with handles on both sides used for cooking the main dish. The main dish gets its name from this pan.

There seems to be general agreement that paella was first made in Valencia, Spain. Today, its popularity is worldwide.

In Spain, ingredients for the dish vary, depending on the locale and on food availability. For example, a paella prepared in an inland town might consist of meat, such as sausage or ham, chicken, and vegetables, while a paella prepared in a coastal village would probably use seafood such as shrimp, clams, lobster, or mussels in place of the meat. (Clams, incidentally, are cooked and served in the shell.) The vegetables used also depend on local supply, but peas, beans, onions, and tomatoes are frequent additions. Other versions may use carrots or artichoke hearts. (See also *Spanish Cookery*.)

International meal-in-one

← Enjoy the flavor of a Spanish dish prepared in your own kitchen. Serve colorful Spanish Paella for an elegant company entrée.

Spanish Paella

¼ cup all-purpose flour
1 teaspoon salt
  Dash pepper
1 2½- to 3-pound ready-to-cook broiler-fryer chicken, cut up
¼ cup olive *or* salad oil
2 carrots, peeled and sliced lengthwise
2 medium onions, quartered
1 celery branch with leaves
2 cups chicken broth
1 clove garlic, crushed
¼ cup diced canned pimiento
½ teaspoon salt
¼ teaspoon ground oregano
¼ teaspoon ground saffron
⅔ cup uncooked long-grain rice
1 9-ounce package frozen artichoke hearts, thawed
¾ pound shelled raw shrimp
12 *small* clams in shells

Combine flour, 1 teaspoon salt, and pepper in plastic or paper bag. Add a few chicken pieces at a time; shake to coat. In heavy skillet brown chicken in hot oil about 20 minutes. Transfer the chicken to a large kettle.

Add next 10 ingredients; simmer, covered, 30 minutes. Add artichoke hearts, shrimp, and clams in shells; simmer, covered, 15 to 20 minutes longer. Makes 6 to 8 servings.

PAIN PERDU *(pä pêr' di)* — The French name for French toast. The literal translation, however, is "lost bread."

PALATABLE *(pal' uh tuh buhl)* — The word used to describe a food that is agreeable or very pleasing to the taste.

PALMETTO — Another name for the cabbage palm. The young, tender leaves of the palmetto are eaten raw or cooked. The pithy hearts of young palmetto stems are often pickled. (See also *Hearts of Palm.*)

PANADA *(puh nä' duh, -nä')* — A traditional European mixture used to bind together forcemeat or stuffings. It is thick, pasty, and has various ingredients, depending on the food with which it is used. One type of panada is made of soft bread crumbs and hot milk; another mixture consists of flour, water, and butter. A third and richer type of panada is a blend of flour, butter, milk, and egg yolks.

PANBROIL — To cook meat, uncovered, in a skillet, removing fat from the pan as it accumulates. Any meat that can be broiled can also be panbroiled.

Pan-Broiled Steak

Select a porterhouse, T-bone, club, sirloin, or tenderloin (filet mignon) steak cut 1 inch thick. Place in a cold heavy skillet. *Do not add shortening* (unless very lean cuts are used). Brown on both sides. Cook, uncovered, over medium-high heat, turning occasionally. Total cooking time is about 9 to 10 minutes for rare, 11 to 12 minutes for medium, and about 20 minutes for well-done. Season, if desired.

PANCAKE — Any of a variety of flat, tender quick breads made from a batter and baked on a griddle or skillet. The thickness of the batter determines whether the pancakes will be thick for hearty eating or thin for easy filling and rolling.

Most probably, the first pancakes evolved from primitive man's effort to dry a mixture of meal and water by spreading it on a flat stone in the sun. Later, Egyptians used a similar method to bake a kind of pancake. Even the men in the Roman legions included pancakes in their diets.

During the Middle Ages, pancakes took on religious significance as pre-Lenten food. It became the custom to eat pancakes on Shrove Tuesday as a means of using up fats before the Lenten fast began and also because the pancake ingredients were symbolic to these people—flour for the staff of life, eggs for fertility, and milk for innocence. This Shrove Tuesday observance may have been patterned after an ancient Roman feast held in the early spring.

The traditional and famous pancake race held on Shrove Tuesday in Olney, England, is said to date from 1445. To win the race, housewives must flip pancakes in a frying pan as they run from the town square to church. The first housewife to the church is the winner. A similar race is run in Liberal, Kansas.

Nutritional value: Pancakes vary in food value, depending on ingredients, but all contain some protein, carbohydrate, and fat from the egg, milk, and flour. A plain 4-inch pancake has 59 calories if made with wheat flour and 47 calories if made with buckwheat flour. The syrups, butter, and other toppings used with the pancakes add considerably more calories.

Types of pancakes: Many types of pancakes are popular in countries around the world. In France they are called crepes; in China *chuen kuen* or egg rolls. They're called *nalesniki* in Poland, blini or *sirniki* in Russia, and blintzes in Central European and Jewish cookery. Sweden has *plattar*, Germany has *Pfannkuchen*, and Hungarians like *palacsinta*.

Characteristics of pancakes: The ingredients used in the pancake batter determine what the final product will be like. Basic pancake ingredients include either wheat flour, buckwheat flour, or cornmeal, plus milk, salt, and leavening. Some recipe variations include fat, sugar, or eggs.

Most of the standard leavening agents are utilized in one type of pancake or another. Soda and buttermilk leaven some; baking powder, others. Yeast leavens buck-

Pour the pancake batter from a shaker container or measuring cup for easy portioning and for pancakes that are uniform in shape.

Burst and unburst bubbles covering the surface as well as slightly dry edges are signs that the pancakes are ready to turn.

Have an urge to flip pancakes? Slip spatula under cake. Give a sudden lift-and-tilt to spatula. Pancake goes up and over.

wheat and sourdough pancakes as well as blinis. Eggs are the leavening agents that make German pancakes so light.

Pancakes are made in all sizes to suit any preference. For the silver dollar-size, only one tablespoon of batter is used, but plate-size pancakes need ¼ cup of batter each. Swedish pancakes take on the size of the shallow depressions of the special platter pan used in their preparation. French crepes have the diameter of the small frying pan in which they are baked.

How to prepare: Techniques for combining pancake ingredients vary with the type of pancake being prepared. Standard pancakes are combined or stirred only enough to blend the ingredients. The small lumps remaining in the batter disappear during baking. If overbeaten, the pancakes are heavy and tough. Some other batters, especially those used for crepes and dainty pancakes made with egg, are beaten until smooth to produce their characteristic textures. Batters made with yeast need to stand for a given time to allow the yeast to leaven the pancakes.

For pancakes in a jiffy, use a convenience pancake product such as plain, buckwheat, or buttermilk-flavored mixes. Most of the convenience mixes need only the addition of liquid and a few stirs or shakes to complete the preparation.

How to cook: To bake pancakes be sure the griddle or skillet is hot enough to make a drop of water dance on the surface. Pour the batter so that the pancakes will not

touch as they expand. Turn them when the tops are bubbly and the edges look slightly dry. Turn the pancakes once only.

German egg pancakes are often cooked in a unique fashion. First, they are partially baked in a skillet on top of the range. Then, they are put into the oven to complete the cooking. When done, the pancakes are high puffs with up-curved edges.

Favorite Pancakes

    1¼ cups sifted all-purpose flour
    1 tablespoon sugar
    3 teaspoons baking powder
    ½ teaspoon salt
        . . .
    1 beaten egg
    1 cup milk*
    2 tablespoons salad oil

Sift together flour, sugar, baking powder, and salt. Combine egg, milk, and salad oil; add to dry ingredients, stirring just till moistened. Using 1 tablespoon or ¼ cup batter for each pancake, bake batter on hot, lightly greased griddle till golden. Turn once. Makes about 12 dollar-size, or eight 4-inch pancakes.

*For thinner pancakes, add an additional 2 tablespoons milk to the batter.

Buttermilk Pancakes

If you like a little tang—

    1¼ cups sifted all-purpose flour
    1 tablespoon sugar
    2 teaspoons baking powder
    ½ teaspoon baking soda
    ½ teaspoon salt
    1 beaten egg
    1 cup buttermilk *or* sour milk
    2 tablespoons salad oil

Sift together all-purpose flour, sugar, baking powder, baking soda, and salt. Combine egg, buttermilk, and salad oil; add to dry ingredients, stirring just till moistened. Using 1 tablespoon or ¼ cup batter for each pancake, bake batter on hot, lightly greased griddle till golden. Turn once. Makes about 12 dollar-size, or eight 4-inch pancakes.

Keeping pancakes hot

If you need to bake pancakes ahead to keep up with your family's demands, pile them on a paper-lined cookie sheet placed in an oven set at its lowest temperature. Place a paper napkin between each layer of pancakes as well as on top of the piles to absorb steam. Crepes can be folded or rolled and reheated in sauce.

Feather Pancakes

    1 cup sifted all-purpose flour
    2 tablespoons sugar
    2 tablespoons baking powder
    ½ teaspoon salt
    1 beaten egg
    1 cup milk
    2 tablespoons salad oil

Sift together dry ingredients. Combine egg, milk, and salad oil; add dry ingredients to liquid, beating till smooth. Bake on hot, lightly greased griddle till golden. Turn once. Makes 12 dollar-size, or eight 4-inch pancakes.

No–Flip Oven Pancakes

    3 eggs
    ½ cup sifted all-purpose flour
    ¼ teaspoon salt
    ½ cup milk
    2 tablespoons butter or
        margarine, melted
    2 tablespoons sugar
    2 tablespoons sliced almonds,
        toasted
    1 tablespoon butter or
        margarine, melted
    1 tablespoon lemon juice

Beat eggs till well blended. Slowly add flour, beating constantly. Stir in salt, milk, and the 2 tablespoons melted butter. Grease 10-inch skillet (handle must be removable or oven-proof). Pour batter into cool skillet.

Bake at 400° for 15 minutes. Remove from oven; quickly sprinkle with sugar and nuts. Combine 1 tablespoon butter and lemon juice; quickly drizzle over all. Serve at once. Serves 2.

How to serve: When pancakes are mentioned, two of the first toppings that come to many peoples' minds are butter pats and maple syrup. Yet, pancakes can take on new faces for breakfast, lunch, and dinner by using simple recipe alterations and different accompaniments. Instead of standard pancakes at breakfast, make buckwheat pancakes and serve them with corn syrup. For a brunch idea, use flavored butters and fruit syrups in place of the traditional flavorings. Or for supper, fill crepes with meat filling for the entrée or fruit-cream cheese filling for dessert, then heat them in a complementary sauce. (See *Bread, Syrup* for additional information.)

Pancake Toppers

Whipped Butter: Beat ½ cup butter with electric mixer till light and fluffy.
Orange Butter: Beat 1 tablespoon confectioners' sugar and ¼ teaspoon grated orange peel into Whipped Butter.
Cranberry-Orange Butter: Place 1 small unpeeled orange, diced; ¼ cup raw cranberries; and ¼ cup sugar in electric blender. Cover; blend 40 seconds. Fold into Whipped Butter.
Blueberry Sauce: In a saucepan cook and stir one 16-ounce can blueberries and 2 teaspoons cornstarch till mixture thickens and bubbles. Stir in 1 teaspoon lemon juice.
Orange Syrup: In a saucepan combine ½ cup butter, 1 cup sugar, and ½ cup frozen orange juice concentrate. Bring to boil; stir.

Bread Crumb Pancakes

     2 slices dry bread
 1½ cups buttermilk *or* sour milk
     2 eggs
     2 tablespoons salad oil
 1½ cups sifted all-purpose flour
     1 teaspoon baking soda
   ½ teaspoon salt

Place bread in blender container. Cover; blend till coarse dry crumbs. Add buttermilk, eggs, salad oil, flour, baking soda, and salt. Cover; blend to combine. Drop by tablespoons onto hot, lightly greased griddle. Bake till golden. Turn once. Makes 2 dozen 4-inch pancakes.

Quick Cottage Cheese Pancakes

Dressed-up with oranges and coconut—

 1½ cups milk
     1 egg
   ¾ cup cream-style cottage cheese
 1½ cups pancake mix
     2 tablespoons butter or
          margarine, melted
     1 teaspoon shredded orange peel
       Orange slices
       Shredded coconut

Place milk, egg, and cottage cheese in blender container; cover container and switch blender on and off 3 or 4 times, till cottage cheese is in small pieces. (Or beat with mixer.) Pour into a bowl. Add pancake mix, stirring just till moistened. Stir in butter or margarine and the 1 teaspoon shredded orange peel.

Bake on hot, lightly greased griddle, using ¼ cup batter for each. Turn once. Serve with oranges and coconut. Makes 12 pancakes.

Jam-Filled Crepes

Gourmet flavor for Sunday brunch—

     1 tablespoon brandy
   ¾ cup apricot *or* peach jam
   ¾ cup sifted all-purpose flour
     2 tablespoons granulated sugar
       Dash salt
     1 cup milk
     2 eggs
       Confectioners' sugar

Stir brandy into jam; set aside. Sift flour, granulated sugar, and salt into mixing bowl. Add milk and eggs; beat till smooth.

Heat a 6- or 7-inch skillet till drop of water dances on surface (375°). Grease lightly. Pour in 2 tablespoons batter; lift pan and tip from side to side so batter covers bottom. Return to heat; cook till underside is lightly browned. Remove to towel-covered tray.

Spread unbrowned side of each crepe with 1 tablespoon of jam mixture; roll up. Repeat with remaining batter and jam. Arrange in a shallow, ovenproof serving dish. Place in 250° oven to keep warm. Sprinkle with confectioners' sugar just before serving. Makes 12 pancakes.

Blueberry Pancakes

Serve with orange-flavored butter—

   1 cup fresh, frozen, or canned
      blueberries
   1 well-beaten egg
   1 cup milk
   ¼ cup butter or margarine,
      melted
   1 cup sifted all-purpose flour
2½ teaspoons baking powder
   2 tablespoons sugar
   ¾ teaspoon salt

Thaw frozen berries; drain frozen or canned blueberries thoroughly. Combine egg, milk, and butter. Sift together flour, baking powder, sugar, and salt; gradually add to egg mixture, beating with electric or rotary beater. Use ¼ cup measure to drop batter on hot, lightly greased griddle. Sprinkle about 2 tablespoons berries over each cake. When underside is golden, turn and brown other side. Makes 8.

Apple Pancakes

Subtle fruit flavor—

   2 cups sifted all-purpose flour
   2 tablespoons sugar
   4 teaspoons baking powder
   1 teaspoon salt
       . . .
   2 well-beaten egg yolks
   2 cups milk
   2 tablespoons butter or
      margarine, melted
   1 cup finely chopped apple
   2 stiffly beaten egg whites
     Butter or margarine
     Confectioners' sugar

Sift together flour, sugar, baking powder, and salt. Combine egg yolks and milk. Pour into dry ingredients; stir well. Stir in 2 tablespoons melted butter and apple. Fold in egg whites. Let batter stand a few minutes.

   Bake on hot, lightly greased griddle, using ⅓ cup batter for each. (Use a spatula to spread batter evenly.) Dot each pancake with butter or margarine. Sprinkle with confectioners' sugar; roll up. Makes 12 pancakes.

Double-Corn Cakes

   1 cup pancake mix
   1 cup cornmeal
   1 teaspoon baking powder
   2 slightly beaten eggs
   1 16-ounce can cream-style corn
   1 cup milk
   2 tablespoons salad oil *or*
      melted shortening

Stir together dry ingredients. Combine eggs, corn, milk, and oil; add to dry ingredients, stirring just till moistened. Bake batter on hot, lightly greased griddle or skillet, using ¼ cup batter for each. Turn once. Makes about sixteen 4-inch pancakes.

Hawaiian Pancakes

   1 20-ounce can pineapple tidbits
   2 tablespoons cornstarch
   ⅓ cup orange juice
   ⅓ cup honey
   2 tablespoons butter or margarine
1½ cups sifted all-purpose flour
   3 tablespoons baking powder
   3 tablespoons sugar
   ¾ teaspoon salt
   2 beaten eggs
1½ cups milk
   3 tablespoons salad oil

Drain pineapple, reserving syrup; add enough water to reserved syrup to make 1 cup. Blend syrup with cornstarch in saucepan. Add pineapple, orange juice, honey, and butter. Cook, stirring constantly, till thickened and bubbly. Keep warm while preparing pancakes.

   For pancakes sift together flour, baking powder, sugar, and salt. Combine eggs, milk, and salad oil; add liquid to dry ingredients, beating till smooth. Bake on hot, lightly greased griddle. Turn once. Serve pineapple sauce over pancakes. Makes twelve 4-inch pancakes.

Tempting stack of hot cakes

There's plenty of golden pineapple-studded →
sauce to grace each serving of these delicious feather-light Hawaiian Pancakes.

Pumpkin Puff Pancakes

Enhanced by an apple cider syrup—

1 cup sifted all-purpose flour
1 tablespoon granulated sugar
2 teaspoons baking powder
½ teaspoon salt
½ teaspoon ground cinnamon

. . .

1 cup milk
½ cup canned pumpkin
2 slightly beaten egg yolks
2 tablespoons butter *or* margarine, melted

. . .

2 stiffly beaten egg whites
Hot Cider Sauce

Sift together flour, sugar, baking powder, salt, and cinnamon. Combine milk, pumpkin, egg yolks, and melted butter or margarine. Add to dry ingredients, stirring just till flour is moistened. Fold in stiffly beaten egg whites. Using about ⅓ cup batter for each pancake, bake on hot, lightly greased griddle. Turn once. Serve with Hot Cider Sauce. Makes 8 pancakes.

Hot Cider Sauce: In saucepan combine ¾ cup apple juice *or* cider, ½ cup brown sugar, ½ cup light corn syrup, 2 tablespoons butter or margarine, ½ teaspoon lemon juice, ⅛ teaspoon ground cinnamon, and ⅛ teaspoon ground nutmeg. Bring to boiling; simmer about 15 minutes. Makes 1¼ cups sauce.

Apple-Sauced Potato Cakes

Quick version of German potato pancakes—

1 3-ounce envelope potato pancake mix
1 cup chopped canned luncheon meat
Applesauce
Ground cinnamon

Prepare potato pancake mix according to package directions. Add luncheon meat. Using about 2 tablespoons batter for each cake, drop batter onto a hot, greased griddle. Bake till golden. Turn once. Meanwhile, heat applesauce; dash with cinnamon. Serve warm applesauce with potato cakes. Makes 10 to 12 small pancakes.

Ham and Chicken Stack-Ups

1 cup pancake mix
1 slightly beaten egg
1 cup milk
2 tablespoons salad oil
1 5-ounce can boned chicken, drained and cut up
1 3-ounce can chopped mushrooms, drained (about ½ cup)
1 10½-ounce can condensed cream of mushroom soup
1 4½-ounce can deviled ham
½ cup dairy sour cream

Combine pancake mix, egg, milk, and oil in mixing bowl; beat with rotary beater till smooth. Using 2 tablespoons batter for each, bake batter on hot, lightly greased griddle, making 12 pancakes. Turn once. Keep pancakes warm.

Place 4 pancakes in bottom of 11¾x7½x1¾-inch baking dish. Combine chicken, drained mushrooms, and *half* the soup. Spread evenly over pancakes in baking dish. Top each with second pancake; spread evenly with deviled ham. Top with remaining 4 pancakes.

Combine remaining soup with sour cream. Spoon over pancake stacks. Bake at 350° till heated through, 10 to 15 minutes. Serves 4.

Ham and Chicken Stack-Ups combine convenience products—pancake mix, canned chicken, mushrooms, and deviled ham.

Swedish Pancakes

3 eggs
1¼ cups milk
¾ cup sifted all-purpose flour
1 tablespoon sugar
½ teaspoon salt

• • •

Butter or margarine, melted
Sugar
Lingonberry Sauce (See
Lingonberry)

Beat eggs till thick and lemon-colored. Stir in milk. Sift together dry ingredients; add to egg mixture, mixing till smooth. Drop by tablespoons onto moderately hot, buttered griddle (or use special Swedish griddle). Spread batter evenly to make thin cakes. Turn when underside is light brown. Spoon melted butter over each cake; sprinkle with sugar. Stack. Pass Lingonberry Sauce. Makes about 52 pancakes.

Mincemeat Pancakes

1¼ cups sifted all-purpose flour
1 tablespoon sugar
3 teaspoons baking powder
½ teaspoon salt
1 beaten egg
1 cup milk
2 tablespoons salad oil *or*
melted shortening
½ cup prepared mincemeat
Apple Syrup

Sift together flour, sugar, baking powder, and salt. Combine egg, milk, and salad oil. Add to dry ingredients along with the mincemeat. Stir just till flour is moistened. Using 2 tablespoons batter for each, bake batter on hot, lightly greased griddle. Serve with Apple Syrup. Makes about ten 4-inch pancakes.

Apple Syrup: In saucepan combine ½ of one 12-ounce can frozen apple cider concentrate, thawed (¾ cup); ¾ cup water; 4 inches stick cinnamon, broken in pieces; and 12 whole cloves. Bring to boiling; reduce heat and simmer 10 minutes. Strain to remove spices. Return syrup to same pan; stir in ½ cup sugar and ¼ cup light corn syrup. Bring to boiling; cook 5 minutes more. Remove from heat; stir in 2 tablespoons butter or margarine. Serve warm.

Super Strawberry Pancakes

Thaw four 10-ounce packages frozen strawberries; drain thoroughly. Prepare Swedish Pancakes as directed, *except* use 2 tablespoons batter for each pancake. Fill each pancake with a spoonful of strawberries and roll up. Arrange 3 pancakes on each plate. Sift confectioners' sugar over pancakes. Top with dollop of whipped cream and a strawberry. Serves 8 or 9.

Jiffy Orange Pancakes

1 beaten egg
1 cup light cream
¼ cup frozen orange juice
concentrate
1 cup pancake mix
Orange Syrup (See page 1553)

Combine egg, cream, and orange juice concentrate. Add pancake mix; stir to remove most lumps. Using about 2 tablespoons batter for each, drop batter onto hot, lightly greased griddle. Bake till golden, turning once. Serve with Orange Syrup. Makes about 18 pancakes.

Pancakes à la Mode

1¼ cups sifted all-purpose flour
¾ teaspoon baking soda
½ teaspoon ground cinnamon
½ teaspoon ground ginger
¼ teaspoon ground nutmeg
¼ teaspoon salt
½ cup light molasses
¼ cup butter or margarine,
melted
1 slightly beaten egg
Vanilla ice cream
Maple-flavored syrup
Chopped pecans

Sift together first 6 ingredients. Combine ⅔ cup water, molasses, butter, and egg; gradually add molasses mixture to flour mixture, blending just till smooth.

Using 2 tablespoons batter for each pancake, bake on medium-hot, lightly greased griddle for 3 to 4 minutes, turning once. Overlap two pancakes on each plate; top with scoop of ice cream, then syrup and nuts. Serves 6 to 8.

Elegant Cherry-Sauced Pancakes are cooked to a golden brownness, then filled with warm cherry sauce. A sugar-lemon juice glaze and additional cherry sauce complete this dessert.

Cherry-Sauced Pancakes

- 1 cup sifted all-purpose flour
- 2 tablespoons sugar
- 3 teaspoons baking powder
- ¼ teaspoon salt
- 1 beaten egg yolk
- 1¼ cups milk
- 1 tablespoon butter, melted
- 1 stiffly beaten egg white
- 6 tablespoons butter, melted
- Cherry Sauce
- ¼ cup sugar
- 1 tablespoon lemon juice

In bowl sift together first 4 ingredients. Combine egg yolk and milk. Gradually add to flour mixture; mix. Stir in 1 tablespoon butter; fold in egg white. Pour scant ⅓ cup batter into hot, lightly greased 8-inch skillet; lift and tilt skillet to spread batter. Cook till underside is golden. Turn; brown other side. Repeat, making 8 cakes in all. Drizzle scant 1 tablespoon butter and spoon 2 tablespoons Cherry Sauce over each cake. Roll as for jelly roll.

Place in 10x6x1¾-inch baking dish. Combine ¼ cup sugar and lemon juice; pour over cakes. Broil 4 inches from heat till sugar dissolves and becomes glossy, 3 to 4 minutes. Pass remaining hot Cherry Sauce. Makes 4 servings.

Cherry Sauce: Thaw and drain one 20-ounce can frozen red sour cherries, reserving 1 cup juice. In saucepan combine 4 teaspoons cornstarch and ¼ cup sugar. Gradually stir in reserved juice. Cook over medium heat, stirring constantly, till thickened and bubbly; cook 1 minute more. Add cherries and few drops red food coloring; heat through.

PANDOWDY—A molasses-sweetened (maple syrup in Vermont) deep-dish, apple dessert with a biscuit crust. Traditionally, the crust is broken up with the serving spoon and stirred into the apple filling before the dessert is served. Pandowdy is usually served warm, with poured-on heavy cream, or with clear lemon or creamy hard sauce.

Apple Pandowdy

Delicious served warm—

> ½ cup sifted all-purpose flour
> ¼ teaspoon salt
> 3 tablespoons shortening
> 4 to 5 teaspoons cold water
> . . .
> ⅓ cup sugar
> ½ teaspoon ground cinnamon
> ¼ teaspoon salt
> ¼ teaspoon ground nutmeg
> ¼ cup molasses
> ½ cup water
> 5 cups peeled, sliced apples
>   (about 5 apples)
> 2 tablespoons butter or margarine
>   Light cream

To make pastry, mix flour and salt together; cut in shortening. Add 4 to 5 teaspoons water, a teaspoon at a time, blending with a fork until mixture holds together. Chill. On floured surface, roll ⅛ inch thick.

Mix sugar, cinnamon, salt, and nutmeg together; add molasses and ½ cup water. Arrange apples in 1½-quart baking dish; pour molasses mixture over. Dot with butter or margarine; cover with pastry, pressing edges to rim of casserole. Bake at 425° for 40 minutes. Remove from oven; chop mixture with knife, being sure piecrust is thoroughly mixed with apples. Bake at 325° till apples are tender, about 20 to 30 minutes. Serve with light cream. Serves 6.

PANFRY—To cook vegetables, fish, or tender cuts of meat in a skillet, using just enough fat to keep the pieces from sticking to the pan. When panfrying, cook the food over moderately high heat, using a heavy frying pan, until the food is browned on both sides.

Pan-Fried Papaya Rings

Peel 1 large, firm papaya. Cut in eight ½-inch crosswise slices; remove seeds. Heat 2 tablespoons butter till bubbly; add fruit and cook quickly, about 1 minute on each side. Sprinkle with lemon juice. Makes 4 servings.

Pan-Fried Tomatoes

Cut unpeeled *green* tomatoes in ½-inch slices. Dip into mixture of flour, salt, and pepper. Fry slowly in small amount of hot fat until browned. Turn and brown tomatoes on other side.

For *ripe* tomatoes, dip ½-inch slices into beaten egg mixed with water, then crumbs. Fry quickly in hot fat; season with salt and pepper.

Pan-Fried Round Steak

Cut 1½ pounds beef round steak, ½ inch thick, into 5 pieces. Use instant meat tenderizer according to label directions. *Do not use salt.* Coat meat immediately with all-purpose flour. Cook quickly in small amount hot shortening just till browned; turn occasionally. Makes 5 servings.

Fried Mullet Parmesan

> 6 fresh or frozen pan-dressed
>   mullet or other fish
>   (about ½ pound each)
> ½ cup all-purpose flour
> ⅛ teaspoon garlic salt
> 1 beaten egg
> ¼ cup milk
> 1 cup fine saltine cracker crumbs
> ¼ cup grated Parmesan cheese
> 2 tablespoons snipped parsley
>   Shortening

Thaw frozen fish. Dry fish thoroughly. Coat fish with a mixture of flour and garlic salt. Dip into a mixture of egg and milk; then roll in a mixture of crumbs, cheese, and parsley. Heat small amount of shortening in large skillet. Place fish in skillet in single layer. Fry over medium heat till browned on one side, 4 to 5 minutes. Turn; fry till fish browns and flakes easily when tested with a fork, 4 to 5 minutes more. Drain. Makes 6 servings.

PANNHAAS, PAWN HASE (*pän' häs*)—Pennsylvania Dutch name for the meat and cornmeal combination usually called scrapple. (See *Pennsylvania Dutch Cookery, Scrapple* for additional information.)

PANNED—Fruit or vegetables, such as cabbage or sliced carrots, cooked in a tightly covered skillet. They steam from their own juices, with butter and seasonings added.

Vegetable Medley

  2 tablespoons salad oil
  2 cups small fresh cauliflowerets
    •   •   •
  2 10-ounce packages frozen peas
½ teaspoon salt
    Dash pepper
  2 tablespoons chopped canned
      pimiento

Heat oil in skillet. Add cauliflowerets and cook, covered, over low heat 10 to 12 minutes, stirring occasionally. Add frozen peas, salt, and pepper; cover and cook 10 minutes longer, separating peas with fork, if necessary. Stir in chopped pimiento. Season to taste with salt and pepper. Makes 8 servings.

Panned Cabbage Slaw

  1 slice bacon
  2 tablespoons finely chopped onion
  1 tablespoon vinegar
  1 tablespoon water
1½ teaspoons sugar
¼ teaspoon salt
    Dash pepper
  2 cups shredded cabbage
  1 small apple, peeled and
      finely chopped
¼ cup dairy sour cream

In small skillet fry bacon till crisp; drain, reserving drippings. Crumble bacon. Add onion to drippings and cook 2 minutes. Stir in vinegar, water, sugar, salt, and pepper. Bring just to boiling. Add cabbage and apple; toss to coat. Cover and cook over medium heat till cabbage just wilts, 5 minutes. Stir in sour cream and top with bacon. Serves 2 or 3.

Herbed Cabbage Medley

  1 medium onion, thinly sliced
  2 tablespoons butter or margarine
½ small head cabbage, shredded
      (3 cups)
  3 medium carrots, shredded
      (about 1 cup)
½ teaspoon salt
¼ teaspoon dried oregano
      leaves, crushed

In medium skillet or saucepan cook onion in butter for 5 minutes; stir in cabbage, carrots, and salt. Cover; cook over medium heat for 8 minutes more. Stir in oregano. Serves 4.

PANOCHA (*puh nō' chuh*)—Another spelling for penuche. (See also *Penuche*.)

PAPAIN (*puh pā' in*)—An enzyme found in the juice of green papayas that tenderizes meat by breaking down the protein. Although papain was not commercially extracted until modern times, it was used centuries ago. The Aztecs, for example, rubbed the juice of green papayas on meat to tenderize it. Today, papain is the active ingredient in many tenderizers.

PAPAW, PAWPAW (*pô pô, puh pô'*)—The fruit of a tree native to the southern and midwestern states that is distinguished by

Mound a generous spoonful of sliced fresh strawberries in the center of papaya halves for a delightful Breakfast Cocktail Deluxe.

Serve fresh chilled papaya halves the traditional way with only a slice of lime as an accompaniment for this succulent fruit.

its brilliant purple flowers. The oblong, yellowish fruits are sweet, soft, and creamy in texture, have many seeds, and have a pungent aroma. Another variety looks like a flat, brown banana. Papayas, tropical fruits with different characteristics, are sometimes erroneously called papaws.

PAPAYA (*puh pä' yuh*)—A tropical fruit that looks like a small, pear-shaped melon. The thin, yellowish skin is smooth, and when ripe, the flesh is deep golden and almost buttery. Peppery-tasting black seeds are scattered throughout the center cavity.

Where papayas first grew is not known; however, a few centuries after Spanish explorations of the Pacific area, they were being cultivated there. Today, they grow extensively in Hawaii, California, and other warm southern states.

Papayas contain no starch, and are low in calories—only 77 in one of average size. The flesh is very rich in vitamin C.

When selecting, look for greenish yellow to full yellow papayas that yield slightly when the fruit is gently pressed. Small spots on the ripe papaya skin are signs of ripeness and full flavor, not of spoilage. Ripen green papayas at room temperature, out of direct sunlight. Don't refrigerate until the papaya is fully ripe.

The classic way to serve papaya is also the easiest; just slice chilled ripe fruit in half lengthwise, scoop out seeds, and serve like cantaloupe. Garnish with a lemon or lime wedge to squeeze over the fruit.

When using papaya in other ways, keep preparation and seasonings simple to protect and enhance the fruit's delicate flavor. Although usually served uncooked, it can be cooked successfully by short-cooking methods that heighten flavor, yet preserve texture. The papaya flavor is very compatible with that of citrus fruits, bananas, pineapple, seafood, coconut, chicken, and pork.

The juice of green papayas contains the enzyme papain which is important as a meat tenderizer. (See also *Fruit*.)

Breakfast Cocktail Deluxe

Halve and seed 2 chilled papayas. Sprinkle papayas with 4 teaspoons lime juice. Fill with 1 cup sliced strawberries. Dust lightly with confectioners' sugar. Makes 4 servings.

Accompany Pan-Fried Papaya Rings with slices of crisp bacon or ham for a real breakfast or brunch treat. (See *Panfry* for recipe.)

Papaya-Raspberry Marble

An elegant salad—

1 3-ounce package raspberry-flavored gelatin
2 cups raspberries

. . .

1 envelope unflavored gelatin
    (1 tablespoon)
2 tablespoons lemon juice
1 2- or 2⅛-ounce package
    dessert topping mix
2 3-ounce packages cream
    cheese, softened
2 cups diced peeled papaya

Dissolve raspberry gelatin in 1 cup boiling water; stir in ½ cup cold water. Chill till partially set; fold in raspberries.

Soften unflavored gelatin in ⅔ cup water; dissolve over hot water. Stir in lemon juice; cool. Prepare topping mix according to package directions; beat in cream cheese. Fold in unflavored gelatin. Chill till partially set; fold in papaya. Layer raspberry and papaya mixtures in 7½-cup mold. Swirl with spoon to marble. Chill overnight. Makes 10 servings.

PAPER BAKE CUPS—Fluted paper cups, white or pastel-colored, sized to fit into muffin pans. They are used for baking cupcakes, muffins, and individual fruitcakes, or for shaping individual frozen salads and desserts. When carrying cupcakes or muffins in a lunchbox or on a picnic, leave the bake cups on.

PAPER COOKERY—A method of retaining flavor and aroma by enclosing food, such as meat, fish, or vegetables, in paper before cooking or baking. When the food is prepared and served in the paper packet, with a crisscross cut in top and with flaps folded back, it is called "en papillote."

Make-ahead favorite

←Papaya-Raspberry Marble, a shimmery molded salad that complements any dinner entreé, is a swirled red and white mixture.

Pompano En Papillote

6 fresh or frozen pompano fillets
    or other fish fillets
3 cups water
1 teaspoon salt
2 lemon slices
1 bay leaf
⅛ teaspoon dried thyme leaves,
    crushed
Parchment paper

. . .

½ cup finely chopped onion
1 clove garlic, minced
2 tablespoons butter or margarine
3 tablespoons all-purpose flour
¼ teaspoon salt
2 slightly beaten egg yolks
2 tablespoons dry white wine
    (optional)
1 7½-ounce can crab meat, drained,
    flaked, and cartilage removed
4 ounces shelled shrimp, cooked
    and chopped (⅔ cup)
1 3-ounce can sliced
    mushrooms, drained

Thaw frozen fish fillets. Bring water, 1 teaspoon salt, lemon, bay leaf, and crushed thyme to boiling. Add fish and poach till fish flakes easily when tested with a fork, about 15 minutes. Remove fish, reserving stock. Cut 6 pieces parchment or brown paper into heart shapes, about 12x9 inches each. Place one fillet on half of each parchment heart.

Strain stock, reserving 1½ cups. In saucepan cook onion and garlic in butter till tender. Blend in flour and ¼ teaspoon salt. Add reserved stock. Cook and stir till thickened and bubbly. Gradually stir small amount of hot mixture into beaten egg yolks; return to hot mixture. Cook and stir over low heat till mixture bubbles. Stir in wine, if desired. Stir in crab, chopped shrimp, and the drained, sliced mushrooms; heat the mixture thoroughly.

Spoon about ½ cup sauce over each fillet. Fold other half of each paper heart over fillet to form individual cases. Seal, starting at top of heart, by turning edges up and folding, twisting tip of heart to hold case closed. Place cases in shallow baking pan. Bake at 400° for 10 to 15 minutes. Cut cases open with large X cut on top; fold back each segment. Transfer paper cases to dinner plates. Makes 6 servings.

PAPRIKA—The red condiment made by grinding dried pods of the mild Capsicum pepper. The Capsicums are native to South America, and many varieties were grown by the pre-Inca peoples of the Andes Mountains. Long before Columbus discovered the Americas, the cultivation of Capsicums had spread to Mexico and Central America. Spanish explorers liked the peppers they found in America, and are credited with introducing Capsicum peppers to the European countries.

The Hungarians are credited with giving paprika its name, which means Turkish pepper. The Turks brought the sweet, mild peppers to Hungary in the sixteenth century. Today, paprika peppers are grown commercially in Hungary, in other Central European areas, and in Spain, Portugal, South America, and California.

Paprika is ground from sweet and mild red peppers that are sun-dried in Europe or kiln-dried in America. For some very mild types, the white pith and seeds are removed before processing. To give a deeper flavor to other types without a real bite, only the stem is removed.

Hungarian paprika is made from special peppers that give a deep, rose red color. Its flavor has somewhat more warmth than that of the brighter red Spanish paprika. Most of the paprika on the spice shelves in American supermarkets is of the mild Spanish type, but imported Hungarian paprika can often be found in specialty and gourmet food stores.

The red color of paprika is due to the presence of certain forms of carotene, a substance related to vitamin A. Paprika was also discovered to be especially rich in vitamin C—even higher in content than is lemon juice. The Hungarian scientist, Professor Albert Szent-Györgyi, was awarded a Nobel prize for his discoveries of how paprika helps maintain health.

Many people discover paprika first as an attractive garnish to sprinkle on foods. Its bright color and mild, sweet taste enhance many foods. Damp romaine or lettuce leaves dipped into paprika make a pretty border for a salad plate. Fish and casseroles benefit from a dash of paprika, too. Even sandwiches, such as the following recipe are attractive with paprika.

Chicken Open-Face Sandwiches

Mix 2 tablespoons all-purpose flour, 1 tablespoon sugar, 1 teaspoon dry mustard, ½ teaspoon salt, and dash cayenne; stir in 2 slightly beaten egg yolks and ¾ cup milk. Cook and stir over very low heat till thick and bubbly. Stir in 3 tablespoons vinegar; chill.

Drain and slice one 5-ounce can water chestnuts. Roll edges of a few chestnuts in paprika; set aside. Spread 8 slices whole wheat bread with some of the dressing; top *each* slice with 5 sprigs watercress, 1 slice cooked chicken, and a few remaining water chestnut slices. Top with a few slices paprika-edged water chestnuts. Pass remaining dressing. Makes 8 servings.

The contributing food value and the flavorful, yet not overpowering taste of paprika, make it worthy of even more generous use. In Hungarian fashion, use one or two tablespoons in goulash, or paprika-style veal. Use a teaspoon to give rich color to French dressing. Be equally generous with paprika in cheese sauces, mayonnaise, and sour cream. (See also *Spice*.)

Paprika Chicken

⅓ cup all-purpose flour
1 teaspoon salt
   Dash pepper
1 2½- to 3-pound ready-to-cook
      broiler-fryer chicken, cut up
¼ cup shortening
      · · ·
½ cup chopped onion
¼ cup water
1 tablespoon paprika
   Sour Cream Gravy

Combine flour, salt, and pepper. Coat chicken pieces with flour mixture. Brown chicken in shortening. Add onion, water, and paprika. Cover tightly; simmer about 45 minutes. Remove chicken pieces and keep hot. Serve with Sour Cream Gravy. Makes 4 servings.

Sour Cream Gravy: Blend 1 tablespoon all-purpose flour and ¼ teaspoon salt into pan juices. Add ½ cup milk and ½ cup dairy sour cream, stirring constantly till thickened and heated. Serve over chicken pieces.

PARAFFIN—A white, waxy substance. Paraffin is tasteless, odorless, harmless to food, and is not easily affected by chemicals in food. Paraffin also makes paper waterproof, as in the household stand-by, waxed paper. In the home, paraffin primarily is used in making candles and for forming a seal over homemade jellies.

Paraffin for use in making jelly and candles is available in food stores. These packages give directions for handling the wax. Usually, paraffin is melted over water or very low heat since it has a low smoking point and is flammable when overheated. The hot paraffin is poured over hot jelly in scalded jars to a depth of ⅛ inch; tip to seal edge. This layer forms a seal to keep air out and prevent spoilage.

PARBOIL—To precook foods briefly in boiling water. Vegetables such as green peppers and potatoes are among the foods that are parboiled. After the precooking, these foods are combined with other ingredients to complete the cooking process.

PARCHED CORN—Dried corn kernels. Parched corn was originally prepared over an open fire to remove the moisture. Ground, parched cornmeal was taken on hunting trips by Indians and early settlers. Today, parched corn kernels, are found in some food shops.

PARE—To cut off the skin or the peel of fruits and vegetables. Paring, also called peeling, is done with the small paring knife, or vegetable scraper or peeler.

PAREVE *(pär' uh vuh)*—A food made without either meat or dairy ingredients. This term is used in Jewish cookery.

PARFAIT *(pär fā')*—1. A frozen dessert that is rich in cream and eggs. 2. A cold, layered dessert served in parfait glasses.

Perfect for summer

Combine the flavors of fresh fruit for Honeydew-Berry Parfait. (See *Melon* for recipe.) Layer fruit with banana-yogurt mixture.

Parfait is the French word for perfect. Certainly, the French frozen type, as well as the many-layered parfait best known in America, makes a perfect dessert.

French parfaits are made by beating a hot syrup into egg yolks until thick. The cooled mixture, blended with whipped cream, is frozen, without stirring, in plain molds or parfait glasses. Unlike the American type, French parfaits have a single flavor. The original parfaits were coffee-flavored, but now, other flavors such as chocolate are substituted for coffee.

The variety of layered parfaits that Americans make is almost endless. Ice cream, pudding, gelatin, or whipped cream is layered with fruit, fruit sauce, or nuts. Ingredients are chosen with emphasis on a tasty flavor and an attractive color combination. Your choice of ingredients depends on personal taste.

Parfaits are an easy dessert to serve when you choose layers that will refrigerate or freeze well. Make them ahead and store in the freezer or refrigerate till time for dessert. (See also *Dessert*.)

Plum Parfaits

　1 pound purple plums
　1 tablespoon cornstarch
　¾ cup sugar
　　Dash salt
　　　• • •
　　Dash ground cinnamon
　　Dash ground cloves
　1 tablespoon lemon juice
　　Vanilla ice cream

Rinse plums; slice, removing pits. Measure 3 cups. Combine cornstarch, sugar, and salt in saucepan. Stir in plums, cinnamon, cloves, and lemon juice. Cover and bring to boil. Simmer 8 to 10 minutes; cool. Layer with vanilla ice cream in parfait glasses. Makes 4 to 6 servings.

Plum delicious

← Take advantage of purple plums in season to make a sauce sparked with spices. Layer the sauce with ice cream for Plum Parfaits.

Cherry-Creme Parfaits

　1 cup whipping cream
　3 tablespoons sugar
　1 teaspoon vanilla
　　Dash salt
　1 cup dairy sour cream
　1 21-ounce can cherry pie filling

Whip the cream with sugar, vanilla, and salt. Fold in sour cream. Alternate layers of cherry pie filling and whipping cream mixture in parfait glasses. Chill. Serves 8 to 10.

Quick Pudding Parfaits

　1 3- or 3¼-ounce package *regular* vanilla pudding mix
　1¾ cups milk
　1 cup whipping cream
　1 teaspoon vanilla
　2 cups sliced strawberries, chilled

Prepare pudding according to package directions, *using 1¾ cups milk*. Chill. Whip the cream. Beat pudding till smooth. Fold whipped cream and vanilla into pudding. Alternate berries and pudding in parfait glasses. Serves 6.

Lime-Berry Parfaits

　1 3-ounce package lime-flavored gelatin
　1 cup boiling water
　1 8-ounce package cream cheese, softened
　⅓ cup sugar
　¼ cup orange juice
　½ teaspoon grated lime peel
　3 tablespoons lime juice
　1 cup whipping cream
　1 10-ounce package frozen red raspberries, thawed

Dissolve gelatin in boiling water. Beat together cream cheese and sugar. Gradually add gelatin, orange juice, lime peel, and lime juice to cream cheese mixture, beating till smooth. Chill till slightly thickened. Whip cream; fold into lime mixture. Chill till partially set. Alternate gelatin mixture and raspberries with syrup in parfait glasses. Makes 6 servings.

Quick Cherry-Cream Parfaits

Vary the flavor of the pudding mix and the pie filling to suit your fancy—

 1 cup milk
 1 cup dairy sour cream
 ¼ teaspoon almond extract
   .   .   .
 1 3⅝- or 3¾-ounce package
  instant vanilla pudding mix
 1 21-ounce can cherry pie
  filling (2 cups)
   .   .   .
 Toasted slivered almonds

In mixer bowl combine milk, sour cream, and almond extract. Add pudding mix; beat with rotary or electric beater till creamy and well blended, about 2 minutes. Fill parfait glasses with alternate layers of pudding, cherry pie filling, and toasted slivered almonds; chill. Garnish with additional almonds. Serves 6.

To make perfect layers for Quick Cherry-Cream Parfaits, pipe the vanilla pudding into the glasses with a pastry tube.

Coffee-Mallow Towers

Make crumb layer quickly by using a blender to crush the wafers—

 24 regular marshmallows
  (about 3 cups)
 1 cup water
 1 tablespoon instant coffee
  powder
 1 cup whipping cream
 ½ cup chocolate wafer crumbs

In medium saucepan combine marshmallows, water, and coffee powder. Cook and stir over medium heat till marshmallows melt. Chill till partially set. Whip cream; fold into marshmallow mixture. (If mixture thins, chill about 20 minutes till partially reset.) In parfait glasses, alternate coffee mixture and chocolate crumbs, beginning and ending with coffee mixture; chill. Top with whipped cream and chocolate curls, if desired. Makes 4 servings.

Slant each glass as you put layers into the parfait glasses. This creates an interesting angle in the pudding and crumb layers.

PARFAIT PIE—A single-crust, refrigerated pie characterized by a fruit, ice cream, and gelatin filling. Occasionally, unflavored gelatin is used, but since the pie originated in the United States as a promotion by a flour miller and a manufacturer of fruit-flavored gelatins, a flavored gelatin is generally specified in most recipes.

Parfait means perfect in French, and this is how this assortment of frozen cream, ice cream, and layered fruit desserts is considered—perfect.

These pies are popular also because they are so easy to make. Few ingredients are needed: Besides a nine-inch pie shell, you need only one pint of ice cream, usually vanilla; one 3-ounce package of fruit-flavored gelatin; and one or more cups of fruit. Larger amounts of delicate or mild-flavored fruits are required to make sure that their flavors come through the finished pie when it is served.

To make a parfait pie, dissolve the fruit-flavored gelatin in boiling water, add vanilla ice cream, a few spoonfuls at a time, and fold in the sweetened, cut-up fruit. As the cold ice cream blends into the hot mixture, the ice cream melts and the gelatin begins to set. The pie filling will hold its shape when chilled.

Almost any variety of sweetened fruit, whether fresh, frozen, canned, or dried, can be teamed with an appropriately flavored gelatin. The exception is fresh or frozen pineapple, which contains an enzyme that prevents gelatin from setting. Sometimes, you will match strawberry with fresh strawberries, or you will choose lemon-flavored gelatin for peaches, bananas, or mixed fruits. The fruit may be sliced, diced, mashed, or puréed. Seasonings such as cinnamon, nutmeg, and coffee powder enhance the combination.

Originally, the pie shell that holds this luscious fruit mixture was made of tender, flaky pastry. Today, however, a crumb crust made of graham crackers, vanilla or chocolate wafers, gingersnaps, or cornflakes is often substituted. The pastry crusts and many of the crumb crusts are baked before filling, but some types of crumb crusts do not require baking, so you can make the parfait pie from start to finish without an oven. (See also *Pie*.)

Peach Parfait Pie

3½ cups sliced fresh peaches, sweetened, *or* 1 29-ounce can sliced peaches
1 3-ounce package lemon-flavored gelatin
½ cup cold water
1 pint vanilla ice cream
. . .
1 9-inch *baked* pastry shell, cooled (See *Pastry*)
Whipped cream

If using fresh peaches, let stand about 15 minutes after mixing with sugar. Drain peaches (fresh or canned), reserving syrup.

Add water to syrup to make 1 cup; heat to boiling. Add gelatin; stir till dissolved. Stir in cold water. Add ice cream by spoonfuls to hot liquid. Stir till melted. Chill till mixture mounds slightly when dropped from a spoon. Reserve a few peach slices for a garnish; fold remainder into ice cream-gelatin mixture. Turn into cooled pastry shell. Chill till firm. Top with whipped cream and reserved peaches.

Pumpkin Parfait Pie

1¼ cups fine graham cracker crumbs
¼ cup granulated sugar
6 tablespoons butter or margarine, melted
½ cup brown sugar
4 teaspoons unflavored gelatin
1 teaspoon instant coffee powder
½ teaspoon ground ginger
½ teaspoon ground cinnamon
¼ teaspoon ground nutmeg
1 cup boiling water
1 pint vanilla ice cream
1 cup canned or mashed cooked pumpkin

In a bowl combine graham cracker crumbs, granulated sugar, and melted butter. Press firmly into a 9-inch pie plate. Chill 45 minutes.

Blend brown sugar, gelatin, coffee powder and spices in mixing bowl. Add boiling water; stir to dissolve. Add ice cream by spoonfuls, stirring till melted. Stir in pumpkin. Chill till mixture mounds when spooned, about 5 minutes. Spoon into crust; chill till firm.

Strawberry Parfait Pie

    1 3-ounce package strawberry-
        flavored gelatin
    1 cup boiling water
    ½ cup cold water
    1 pint vanilla ice cream
    1 cup sliced fresh strawberries
    1 9-inch *baked* pastry shell,
        cooled (See *Pastry*)
    Whipped cream

Dissolve gelatin in boiling water. Stir in cold water. Add vanilla ice cream by spoonfuls, stirring till melted. Chill till mixture mounds slightly when spooned. Gently fold in strawberries. Turn into baked pastry shell. Chill till firm. Top with whipped cream. Trim with additional strawberries, if desired.

PARKER HOUSE ROLL—A soft-crusted, yeast-raised dinner roll made by folding a flat round of dough in half. These rolls are named after their place of origin, the Parker House, a restaurant opened in Boston in 1855 by Harvey D. Parker. The rolls, also known as pocketbook rolls, look like small purses after they have been baked.

Pair up fresh strawberries, strawberry-flavored gelatin, and ice cream in a flaky pastry shell for Strawberry Parfait Pie.

Parker House Rolls are luncheon favorites that are simple to shape. Just cut with a round cutter, crease off-center, and fold.

Parker House Rolls

    1 package active dry yeast
    3½ cups sifted all-purpose flour
    1¼ cups milk
    ¼ cup shortening
    ¼ cup sugar
    1 teaspoon salt
            • • •
    1 egg
    Butter

In large mixer bowl combine yeast and *2 cups* of the flour. Heat milk, shortening, sugar, and salt just till warm, stirring occasionally to melt shortening. Add to dry mixture in mixing bowl. Add egg. Beat at low speed with electric mixer for ½ minute, scraping sides of bowl constantly. Beat 3 minutes at high speed.

By hand, stir in enough of the remaining flour to form a soft dough. Place in greased bowl, turning once to grease surface. Cover and let rise till double, about 1½ to 2 hours.

Turn out on lightly floured surface and roll dough ⅜ inch thick. Cut with floured 2½-inch round cutter; lightly brush surface of each circle with butter. Make an off-center crease. Fold so top overlaps slightly; seal end edges of each roll. Cover and let rise till double, 30 to 45 minutes. Bake on greased baking sheet at 400° for 12 to 15 minutes. Makes 3 dozen.

Parmesan cheese is good for grating on pasta dishes.

PARKIN—A British spice cake or gingerbread made of oatmeal flour and sweetened with treacle or golden syrup.

PARMESAN CHEESE (*pär' mi zan'*)—The name for hard, cow's milk cheeses of the grana family, which Italians call Parmigiano Reggiano. This group of cheeses is characterized by its grainy texture when aged. Italian in origin, this cheese was named for the duchy of Parma some time during the twelfth century. It was introduced to France in the mid 1500s by Catherine de Medici. In succeeding centuries the popularity of Parmesan cheese spread rapidly throughout the world.

Although the young cheeses, aged less than 3 months, are soft enough to eat by the piece, most Parmesan cheese, aged one to two years, but not more than four years, is very hard and is most often used in its grated or shredded form. Domestic brands are available either grated or shredded in cartons and jars, while pieces that are cut from domestic and imported varieties are found generally at specialty cheese shops.

Parmesan cheese is a must with pasta, but it is also a favorite in soups such as French onion and Minestrone, in egg dishes, over vegetables, and tossed with crisp cereal as a snack. (See also *Cheese.*)

Parmesan-Rice Squares

In a shallow pan toss 2 cups bite-sized crisp, rice squares in 3 tablespoons melted butter or margarine till coated. Sprinkle with ¼ cup grated Parmesan cheese. Toast the cereal mixture in a 300° oven about 15 minutes, stirring occasionally. Cool before serving.

Parmesan Omelet

    4 egg yolks
    4 egg whites
    ¼ cup grated Parmesan cheese
    1 tablespoon butter or margarine
       Cheddar Cheese Sauce

Beat egg yolks till very thick. Wash beater. Beat egg whites till frothy; add ¼ cup water. Beat till stiff but not dry. Fold yolk mixture into whites. Fold in cheese. Melt butter in a 10-inch oven-going skillet; heat till sizzling hot. Pour in omelet mixture. Reduce heat; cook slowly till puffed and golden on bottom, about 5 minutes. Then, bake at 325° till knife inserted in center comes out clean, about 6 to 8 minutes.

Loosen sides of omelet with spatula. Make shallow crease across omelet at right angles to skillet handle, just above center. Slip spatula under large half nearer handle. Tilt pan. Fold upper (large) half over lower half. Tip omelet onto heated platter. Makes 2 or 3 servings.

Cheddar Cheese Sauce: In saucepan melt 4 teaspoons butter. Blend in 4 teaspoons all-purpose flour and dash salt. Add ¾ cup milk. Cook, stirring constantly, till thick. Remove from heat. Add 3 ounces sharp natural Cheddar cheese, shredded; stir. Spoon over omelet.

PARMIGIANA, PARMIGIANO—The name used to designate foods made with Parmesan cheese. (See also *Italian Cookery.*)

Veal Parmigiana

Melt 3 tablespoons butter or margarine in a 10x6x1¾-inch baking dish. Combine ½ cup cornflake crumbs, ¼ cup grated Parmesan cheese, ½ teaspoon salt, and dash pepper. Cut 1 pound veal cutlets *or* round steak, about ¼ inch thick, into 4 serving-sized pieces; dip steak in 1 slightly beaten egg, then in crumb mixture. Place in baking dish. Bake at 400° for 20 minutes. Turn; bake 15 to 20 minutes.

Meanwhile, in saucepan combine one 8-ounce can (1 cup) tomato sauce, ½ teaspoon dried oregano leaves, crushed; ½ teaspoon sugar; and dash onion salt. Heat to boiling, stirring frequently. Pour tomato sauce over meat. Top with 4 ounces sliced mozzarella cheese. Return casserole to oven to melt cheese. Serves 4.

PARSLEY—A decorative, green-leafed herb of the carrot family used to season and garnish foods. Although once limited to southern Europe where it was used for medicinal purposes as well as for food, parsley is now grown worldwide.

Nutritional value: Although parsley contains a considerable amount of vitamin A, it is usually not eaten in large enough amounts to affect nutrition to any extent. One tablespoon contains only 1 calorie.

Types of parsley: There are three main types of parsley: curled-leafed, Italian, and Chinese. Curled-leafed parsley, as its name implies, has ruffled leaves and is the most popular form for garnishes. Italian parsley on the other hand, has flat leaves that are a darker green and has a more pungent flavor. Because of its flavor, this type of parsley is usually used as a seasoning. Chinese parsley is the leaves of the coriander plant. It looks like the other types of parsley, and oriental cooks use it like curled-leafed parsley to garnish and season the foods that they prepare.

How to select and store: Both fresh and dehydrated parsley are available to consumers throughout the year. When selecting fresh parsley, look for bright green, perky leaves. Dehydrated parsley, found in the spice section, can be substituted for fresh parsley. It does not need to be rehydrated unless the recipe lacks sufficient moisture. Dehydrated parsley flakes are shelf stable, whereas fresh parsley must be refrigerated in a covered container. Wash fresh parsley leaves and shake off the excess moisture. If the leaves are wilted, revitalize them by cutting the stems and standing the parsley in cold water.

How to use: Undoubtedly, parsley is the universal garnish for appetizer, meat, salad, and vegetable dishes. Bushy whole sprigs quickly brighten the serving platter or kitchen-assembled dinner plates. When chopped, a parsley garnish may be sprinkled on as a topping. A colorless food such as an appetizer spread or a pâté is made appealing by rolling the outside of the food in chopped parsley.

Adding parsley flavor to a cooked dish is achieved by using parsley alone or with other seasonings. Dash chopped parsley into a butter sauce, into a butter spread, or into a salad dressing. As a flavor blend, use parsley in a bouquet garni or fines herbes combination. (See *Garnish, Herb* for additional information.)

Parslied Bread Slices

Slice 1 loaf French bread on the diagonal. Spread slices with ½ cup softened butter or margarine. Sprinkle with paprika and ½ cup snipped parsley. Bake on cookie sheet at 350° for 15 to 20 minutes. Serve warm.

Parslied New Potatoes

  1½ **pounds tiny new potatoes**
  ¼ **cup butter or margarine, melted**
  ¼ **cup snipped parsley**
  1 **tablespoon lemon juice**

Scrub or scrape potatoes. Cook in boiling, salted water for 15 to 20 minutes; drain. Peel, if desired. Combine butter, parsley, and lemon juice. Pour over hot potatoes. Serves 4 to 6.

To snip parsley, first rinse and drain it well. Then, place in a container such as a measuring cup, and snip with kitchen shears.

Parslied Potato Salad

    4 cups diced, peeled, cooked
        potatoes
    ¼ cup sliced celery
    3 tablespoons snipped parsley
    2 tablespoons chopped green
        pepper
    2 tablespoons chopped green onion
    2 tablespoons chopped dill pickle
            • • •
    ¾ cup mayonnaise or salad
        dressing
    2 tablespoons clear French-style
        salad dressing with herbs and
        spices
    ¾ teaspoon seasoned salt
    ¼ teaspoon dry mustard
        Dash pepper

Combine potatoes, celery, parsley, green pepper, onion, and pickle; toss lightly. Blend together remaining ingredients; gently fold into
potato mixture. Pack into an 8½x4½x2½-inch
loaf dish; chill. Unmold on lettuce-lined plate;
trim the potato salad with additional parsley,
if desired. Makes 4 or 5 servings.

PARSNIP—A creamy white, carrot-shaped
root vegetable. Parsnips are planted in the
summer vegetable garden, although their
flavor becomes sweeter when the roots
are exposed to temperatures below 40°.
Often, they are not dug up until winter.

Wild forms of parsnips have grown in
western Asia and southern Europe for
centuries. Ancient Greeks and Romans
are known to have eaten the wild forms.
Cultivated parsnips were not well known
in Europe until the 1700s.

Parsnips were introduced to the United
States during the settlement of the early
Virginia colonies. In a turn-about-face, Indians learned of parsnip roots from the
settlers and began cultivating parsnips for
their own food purposes.

Nutritional value: One-half cup of cooked
parsnips provides one vegetable serving
as determined by the Basic Four Food
Groups. This amount contains about 65
calories, mainly from carbohydrates, as
well as many vitamins and minerals.

How to select and store: Parsnips are usually sold by the pound, mainly during late
fall and winter months. Choose roots that
are firm, well-shaped, smooth, and free of
major blemishes. Small- to medium-width
roots have the best texture and flavor.
Avoid overly large or coarse parsnips, or
wilted and flabby ones.

Parsnips need high moisture to retain
freshness, so they should be tightly
wrapped and stored in the vegetable bin
of the refrigerator. If kept properly they
may be held for one to two weeks.

How to prepare and use: Parsnips are first
washed, then scraped or peeled to remove
the outer skin. They may be cooked whole,
halved, or sliced. Cook, covered, in a small
amount of boiling, salted water 25 to 40
minutes for whole parsnips, and 15 to 20
minutes for halves and slices. For a menu
variation, bake them with a beef or pork
roast, or pan- or deep-fat fry them. Sliced
or mashed, parsnips have a delicate flavor
that should not be masked by high seasoning. Most often parsnips are either buttered and seasoned with salt and pepper,
glazed like carrots or sweet potatoes, or
creamed. They are also a delicious addition
to a variety of soups. (See *Carrot, Vegetable* for additional information.)

Extra-Special Parsnips

    12 medium parsnips, peeled, cooked,
        and drained
    1 cup undrained crushed pineapple
    ½ teaspoon grated orange peel
    ½ cup orange juice
    2 tablespoons brown sugar
    2 tablespoons butter or margarine

Split parsnips lengthwise; place in a 10x6x1¾-
inch baking dish. Combine next 4 ingredients
and ½ teaspoon salt; pour over. Dot with butter. Bake at 350° for 30 to 35 minutes, basting
occasionally. Makes 6 servings.

Pan-Fried Parsnips

Drain cooked parsnip halves. Brown in butter.
Season; sprinkle with a little sugar, if desired.

PARTRIDGE—1. A name used in some parts of the United States for the quail. 2. A bird related to the pheasant and quail. This grayish-colored game bird, which is smaller than a pheasant, is characterized by a patch of dark feathers on its breast and by brownish gray tail feathers.

Like most other game birds, the young partridge is best for eating. To keep the partridge's succulent white meat moist and flavorful, lard it or brush it with some fat during cooking. (See also *Game*.)

Partridge in Red Wine

    2 1-pound ready-to-cook partridges,
         cut up
    ½ cup all-purpose flour
    ¼ cup butter or margarine
    2 tablespoons finely chopped onion
    1 10½-ounce can condensed beef
         broth
    ¾ cup claret or red Burgundy

Coat partridges with mixture of flour and 1 teaspoon salt. Brown birds in butter or margarine in Dutch oven. Add onion and broth. Cook, covered, over low heat till tender, about 50 to 60 minutes. Remove birds to serving dish. Add wine to Dutch oven; simmer 5 minutes, stirring up brown bits from bottom of pan. Pour sauce over partridges. Makes 2 or 3 servings.

PASKHA, PASKA (*päsk′ hä*)—A Russian Easter dessert. The essential ingredients in this rich dessert are cottage cheese, butter, candied fruits, and nuts. *Paskha* is molded into the shape of a pyramid and decorated with symbols of the resurrection of Christ. (See also *Russian Cookery*.)

PASSION FRUIT—An egg-shaped fruit grown in tropical and warm temperate climates. This fruit, native to tropical South America, now grows widely in Australia and Hawaii and, to some extent, in California. The two common varieties are the purple and yellow passion fruit.

Reportedly, passion fruit was named by missionaries to South America who thought the flower resembled the crown of thorns and other symbols of Christ's crucifixion. Both the tart-sweet, yellow pulp and the black seeds of the passion fruit are edible. Passion fruit, also called *granadilla*, is delicious eaten fresh as a dessert or cooked in pies, candies, or cakes. The juice of this fruit adds a distinctive flavor to jellies and beverages. (See also *Fruit*.)

PASSOVER BREAD—Another name for the Jewish bread, matzo. (See *Jewish Cookery*, *Matzo* for additional information.)

PASSOVER CAKE—Jewish cake made with potato or matzo flour and served during Passover. (See also *Jewish Cookery*.)

PASSOVER WINE—A sweet wine that is used by the Jewish people during Passover. (See also *Jewish Cookery*.)

PASTA (*pä′ stuh*)—The Italian word for "paste" that has come to mean products in the macaroni, spaghetti, and noodle families. All pasta is made of wheat granules or flour (usually durum wheat) and water.

Legend has it that Marco Polo took macaroni home to Italy from the Orient in the thirteenth century. However, some Italians argue vehemently that ravioli was eaten in Rome well before Polo ever set out on his extended journeys. These Italians are so interested in setting the record straight that they have built a museum, the *Museo Storico degli Spaghetti*, in Pontedassio, near the Italian Riviera.

Thomas Jefferson introduced pasta to the United States. In 1786, he brought back a spaghetti die (metal plate pierced with holes) from Italy. Pasta, however, did not become popular in America until the early part of the twentieth century. Mark A. Carleton, a wheat scientist with the United States Department of Agriculture, brought varieties of durum wheat to this country in 1900, and the growth of the macaroni food industry followed.

Trio of pasta dishes

Treat the family to various pasta recipes: →
Creamy Chicken Casserole, Ham and Mac Bake, or Seasoned Pork Chop Dinner.

The economy and versatility of pasta have made it a mainstay not only in the United States, but throughout the world.

Although not all of the pasta recipes used by American cooks are Italian in origin, the Italian influence is widespread. It is seen especially in the number of Italian names that are present in any pasta recipe collection, and in the retention of the word "pasta" itself.

In the Orient, noodles are second only to rice as a staple food. Oriental noodles come in great variety and are made of wheat, rice, or soybean flour.

The Japanese are fond of *harusame* (bean thread noodles). Along with its many other uses, *harusame* is an essential ingredient in Sukiyaki. Noodles are also very important to the Chinese, with cellophane noodles and dried noodles, often fried till crisp, being the most popular varieties.

Indonesians favor crisp fried noodles in combination with meat sauces. Noodles are also at home in the Philippines in a wide, yellow form called *miti*.

Sometimes called the Greek national dish, *Pastitsio* is a meat-macaroni dish that has a delicious custard topping.

Eastern Europeans also have pasta traditions. In Hungary, noodles run a close second to meat and fish main dishes. A sweet mixture called noodles with poppy seed is a popular Lithuanian dessert.

Scandinavians prefer pasta in the form of macaroni, which they frequently use in cold salads in the smorgasbord.

How pasta is manufactured: While some pasta is still made in the home, most pasta products come from factories. Although they differ in shape and size, most manufactured pastas have one thing in common —durum wheat is their major ingredient. Durum, a hard, spring wheat, is milled into a golden, granular product called semolina, into so-called "granulers" with a higher percentage of flour, or into flour itself. Semolina or granulers is used to make spaghetti and macaroni products, while durum flour is used for making noodles. Durum wheat gives cooked pasta its firmness and presents a starchy residue.

Spaghetti and macaroni are both formed by forcing a flour-wheat dough mixture through the holes in a metal plate (die). As the dough is forced through the spaghetti die, a rack moves against the soft strands and folds them over a carrying rod as a knife cuts them to length.

Macaroni manufacture is similar, except that pins in the openings of the die produce a tubular shape. A revolving knife cuts the macaroni to the proper length. Each macaroni variation has its own special die. For example, "alphabets" are forced through letter-shaped openings.

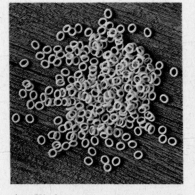

Anellini, meaning "tiny rings," is appropriately named. This small, round pasta is used primarily in a very wide variety of soups and stews.

Conchiglie, shaped like conch shells, is used in many casseroles. *Conchiglioni* and *conchiglietti* are versions of the same pasta shape.

Ravioli, small squares of pasta stuffed with a meat, cheese, or poultry filling, is usually served with a thick and spicy tomato sauce.

Noodle dough is golden-colored because it contains egg or egg solids in addition to flour and water. In the manufacture of noodles, the dough is extruded from machines in the desired width and is then cut to the proper length.

After shaping, all pasta products are dried and weighed before packaging.

Nutritional value: Since pasta holds such a favored position with Italian cooks, people from other countries sometimes express wonder that obesity is not Italy's number one problem. This view arises from the American belief that a serving of pasta is a calorie-laden plate. Actually, an average serving of plain macaroni adds up to just 155 calories and lends a feeling of fullness that discourages overeating. Often, though, calories are added in the form of a sauce, sometimes containing cheese or meat, served with the pasta.

The pasta manufacturer has the option of enriching his pasta by adding specified amounts of calcium and vitamin D. A two-ounce serving of enriched macaroni provides the following percentages of the recommended daily allowances for vitamins and minerals: 25 percent of the thiamine, 12 percent of the riboflavin, 20 percent of the niacin, and 16 percent of the iron. Noodles offer a nutritional bonus because of their egg content.

Types of pasta: The creation of the many different pasta forms has become an art. Stars, shells, flowers, ribbons, wheels, and spirals make pasta cookery a sort of poetry, especially in Italy where most of the shapes originated.

Macaroni—Its use depends upon size.

1. Small, shell-shaped ones are called *maruzzine* (tiny seashells), *ditalini* resemble little thimbles, *coralli* are very small tubes, and *acini di pepe* look like little peppercorns. These dainty bits are used in soups.

2. Medium-sized macaroni range from the well-known elbow type (hollow semicircles) to the less-ordinary creations. Some types are twisted tightly into corkscrew shape, while others resemble small wheels, seashells, or butterflies. These are most often used in baked dishes.

3. Large macaroni are usually prepared with a filling and topped with a sauce. *Ziti* (bridegrooms), *zitoni* (husky bridegrooms), and *tufoli* are all included in this macaroni class.

Spaghetti—A vast array of interesting shapes are available in spaghetti, too. Nested *vermicelli* (little worms) look like thick skeins of delicate strands, *fusili* (twists) have a gay, zigzag crimp, and sweet music is made with spaghetti *alla chitarra* (guitar strings).

Rote, obviously nicknamed "wheels" because of its shape, which includes a tiny hub, spokes, and a rim, is a very popular form of pasta.

Fettuccine verde is quite delicious served as a base for saucy meat dishes. Spinach is added to the dough mixture; hence, its green color.

Vermicelli is a very thin form of spaghetti frequently sold in two forms—long, straight rods and nests or clusters as shown here.

Noodles—The main difference between noodle forms is their widths.

1. *Trenettine* (extra fine) and *trenette* (fine) are the narrowest.
2. *Fettuccelle*, *fettuccine*, and *fettucce* are width gradations of medium-sized noodles.
3. *Lasagnette* (broad) and *lasagne* (extra broad) are the widest.

Other noodle variations are achieved in shape by curling, and in color, as when spinach is added to the dough to produce the colorful *fettuccine verde*.

How to store: Because they are quite low in moisture content, uncooked pasta products have a very long shelf life. They are convenient to keep on hand for everyday family meals. Campers also find them ideal for meals because, in addition to needing no refrigeration before cooking, pasta products are lightweight and are very easy for the cook to pack.

After cooking, pasta casseroles can be stored one or two days in the refrigerator or up to six months in the freezer. The plan-ahead cook can double a pasta recipe and freeze the second meal to enjoy some future busy day.

How to prepare: In this country, most pasta recipes call for packaged pasta, which is a welcome time-saver for homemakers.

But for the experimental cook, a batch of homemade pasta can prove rewarding. In Italy, where an occasion such as a wedding or a christening often calls for a particular pasta, the homemaker takes great pride in preparing her own. However, whether the pasta is homemade or purchased, the following directions apply.

Equipment needed—A large saucepan (at least 5-quart), measuring cups and spoons, a colander, and a slotted spoon are the items needed for pasta cooking.

Method—The water in which pasta products are cooked should be ample and boiling. The boil should not be passive but rather, as some say, "boiling mad." The rolling boil along with the large water supply and an occasional stir keeps the pasta from settling into a clump. Two quarts of water and one tablespoon of salt to each eight ounces pasta is advised.

Cooking time for pasta varies according to the thickness of the variety. A taste test after eight minutes will indicate whether the pasta has reached a stage Italians call *al dente* (to the tooth), which describes a certain desirable firmness. This taste test will also tell you whether there is any starchy flavor, which indicates that the pasta is not sufficiently done.

If pasta is not going directly to the table, hold it in the following manner until serving time. After draining, run cold water

Lasagne, a wide, flat pasta, lends its name to a casserole made of this pasta, several cheeses, and a well-seasoned tomato sauce.

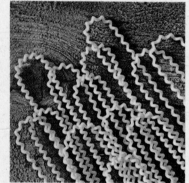

Fusilli, long, thin spaghetti strands twisted like a corkscrew, can be used to give your favorite spaghetti and meatballs an entirely new look.

Manicotti filled with a savory meat, poultry, or cheese mixture and served with a flavorful sauce makes an enticing, good-tasting main dish.

over the pasta quickly. Cover the pasta and hold it until serving time when a brief return to boiling water will bring it back to serving temperature.

There are so many pasta forms available that you can serve a different type every day for months without repeating. Although not every pasta variety is in every market, this should not discourage pasta cookery. If the type of pasta called for in a recipe is not available, you can usually substitute another type for it.

Beef and Macaroni

  1 3½-ounce package sliced smoked
     beef, snipped (1 cup)
  1 15-ounce can macaroni and cheese
  1 3-ounce can chopped mushrooms,
     drained
  2 ounces sharp natural Cheddar
     cheese, shredded (½ cup)
½ cup chopped green pepper
  1 hard-cooked egg, chopped
  1 tablespoon instant minced onion
½ teaspoon Worcestershire sauce
     . . .
  2 tablespoons butter or margarine
½ cup soft bread crumbs

Combine snipped smoked beef, macaroni and cheese, chopped mushrooms, shredded cheese, green pepper, hard-cooked egg, onion, and Worcestershire. Turn into 1-quart casserole.

Melt butter or margarine; mix in soft bread crumbs. Sprinkle buttered crumbs over top of casserole. Bake, uncovered, at 350° for 35 to 40 minutes. Makes 4 servings.

Veal Scallopine

Elegant enough for company—

  1 tablespoon all-purpose flour
½ teaspoon salt
    Dash pepper
  4 veal cutlets (about 1 pound)
¼ cup salad oil
½ medium onion, thinly sliced
  1 16-ounce can tomatoes, cut up
  1 3-ounce can sliced mushrooms,
     undrained
  1 tablespoon snipped parsley
  1 tablespoon capers, drained
¼ teaspoon garlic salt
¼ teaspoon dried oregano leaves,
     crushed
  6 cups water
1½ teaspoons salt
  1 teaspoon salad oil
  4 ounces noodles
  1 tablespoon butter or margarine

In shallow bowl combine all-purpose flour, ½ teaspoon salt, and pepper; coat veal cutlets lightly with flour mixture. In medium skillet brown veal slowly in ¼ cup hot oil. Remove meat from skillet. Add sliced onion to skillet; cook till tender but not brown.

Add cooked veal cutlets, cut-up tomatoes, sliced mushrooms with liquid, snipped parsley, drained capers, garlic salt, and crushed oregano to skillet. Cover and simmer till veal is tender, about 20 to 25 minutes.

To cook noodles, combine water, 1½ teaspoons salt, and 1 teaspoon salad oil in large saucepan; bring to vigorous boil. Add noodles; cook till tender, but still firm. Drain. Add butter; toss together. Arrange veal on hot buttered noodles; top with sauce. Serves 4.

Quick Vegetable Soup

In large saucepan combine two 13¾-ounce cans chicken broth, one 10-ounce package frozen mixed Italian or Spanish vegetables, ⅓ cup catsup, ¼ cup anellini (tiny hollow circles), 2 tablespoons dried celery flakes, 1 tablespoon instant minced onion, and 1 teaspoon dry Italian salad dressing mix. Bring to boiling; reduce heat. Cover and simmer till pasta is tender, 30 minutes. Makes 5 to 6 servings.

Carousel Salad

½ 7-ounce package spaghetti,
 broken, cooked, drained,
 and cooled (about 2 cups)
1 cup shredded carrots
½ cup diced celery
½ cup mayonnaise
2 tablespoons chopped dill pickle
1 teaspoon dill pickle juice
¼ teaspoon dried basil leaves,
 crushed

Combine first 3 ingredients. Blend together remaining ingredients and ½ teaspoon salt. Toss with spaghetti mixture. Chill. Serves 6 to 8.

Chili-Burger Supper

An extra-quick meal-in-a-dish—

In saucepan cook 1 cup elbow macaroni or spaghetti according to package directions; drain thoroughly. Brown 1 pound ground beef in skillet. Add one 11-ounce can condensed chili-beef soup, one 10¾-ounce can condensed tomato soup, and cooked macaroni or spaghetti. Heat, stirring occasionally, till soup-pasta mixture is bubbly, about 5 to 7 minutes.

Halve diagonally 3 slices sharp process American cheese, and overlap cheese triangles atop hot mixture. Cover for a few minutes to melt cheese slightly. Serve at once. Serves 6.

These hearty soups of pasta are cold weather favorites. The Hot Tomato Bouillon (see *Tomato* for recipe) uses *acini di pepe*, and the Quick Vegetable Soup contains *anellini*.

Ham and Mac Bake

       1 6-ounce package elbow macaroni
             (1⅔ cups)
       ¼ cup butter or margarine
       ¼ cup all-purpose flour
       2 tablespoons prepared mustard
       ¼ teaspoon salt
       2 cups milk
       2 tablespoons brown sugar
       2 cups cubed cooked ham
       2 medium apples, pared and
             thinly sliced (2 cups)
       1 cup soft bread crumbs (1¼
             slices bread)
       2 tablespoons butter, melted

Cook macaroni in boiling, salted water just till tender, about 8 to 10 minutes; drain. In large saucepan melt the ¼ cup butter; blend in flour, mustard, salt, and dash pepper. Add milk all at once. Stir in brown sugar. Cook and stir till thickened and bubbly. Stir in cooked macaroni, ham, and apple. Turn into 2-quart casserole. Combine bread crumbs and melted butter; sprinkle over top. Bake at 350° for 30 to 35 minutes. If desired, garnish with unpared poached apple slices. Makes 8 servings.

Creamy Chicken Casserole

       6 ounces occhi di lupo (4 cups)
             or 1 6-ounce package elbow
             macaroni (1⅔ cups)
       2 cups diced cooked chicken
       5 ounces sharp process American
             cheese, shredded (1¼ cups)
       1 10½-ounce can condensed cream
             of chicken soup
       1 cup milk
       1 3-ounce can sliced mushrooms,
             drained
       ¼ cup chopped canned pimiento

Cook occhi di lupo in boiling, salted water till tender, about 15 minutes, stirring occasionally. (Cook elbow macaroni about 6 minutes.) Rinse with cold water; drain. Combine chicken, *1 cup* shredded cheese, soup, milk, mushrooms, pimiento, and pasta. Turn into 2-quart casserole; bake, covered, at 350° for 50 to 60 minutes. Uncover; top with remaining cheese and return to oven till cheese melts. Makes 6 servings.

Seasoned Pork Chop Dinner

       3 cups farfalle (butterfly-
             shaped pasta)
       1 16-ounce can tomatoes
       ¼ teaspoon dried thyme leaves,
             crushed
       6 pork chops, cut ½ inch thick
       ½ cup chopped onion
       1 beef bouillon cube
       ¼ teaspoon dried marjoram leaves,
             crushed
       ½ green pepper, cut in rings
          Paprika

Cook farfalle in boiling, salted water just till tender, about 10 to 12 minutes; drain. Drain tomatoes, reserving ¾ cup juice. Cut tomatoes into quarters; stir into farfalle along with ½ teaspoon salt and crushed thyme. Place in an 11¾x7½x1¾-inch baking dish.

Trim fat from chops. In skillet cook trimmings till 2 tablespoons drippings accumulate. Discard trimmings; add chops and brown. Arrange chops over farfalle. Sprinkle with onion. In small saucepan combine reserved tomato juice, bouillon cube, ½ teaspoon salt, marjoram, and dash pepper. Cook and stir till bouillon is dissolved; pour over chops. Cover and bake at 350° for 1 hour. Remove cover; place green pepper rings over chops. Cover and bake till green pepper is tender, about 15 minutes more. Sprinkle with paprika. Serves 6.

Chicken-Noodle Bake

Cook 8 ounces lasagne noodles in large amount boiling, salted water till tender; drain. Rinse in cold water. In saucepan cook ⅓ cup chopped onion and ⅓ cup chopped green pepper in 2 tablespoons butter till tender. Add one 10½-ounce can condensed cream of mushroom soup, 1 cup milk, and ½ teaspoon poultry seasoning; heat. Beat together two 3-ounce packages cream cheese, softened, and 1 cup cream-style cottage cheese: stir in ¼ cup sliced pimiento-stuffed green olives and ¼ cup snipped parsley.

Dice cooked chicken to make 3 cups. Place *half* the noodles in an 11¾x7½x1¾-inch baking dish; layer with *half* the cheese, *half* the chicken, and *half* the soup. Repeat layers. Top with 1 cup buttered bread crumbs. Bake at 375° for 45 minutes. Let stand. Serves 8.

PASTE—A soft, pliable dough or mixture such as an almond paste.

PASTEURIZATION—A process developed by Dr. Louis Pasteur to make liquids safe to drink by applying sufficient heat to kill harmful bacteria. Pasteurization does not affect flavor or nutritive value.

There are two methods of pasteurization. In the first method, the liquid is held at a temperature of 161° for 15 seconds, while in the second method, the liquid is heated to 143° for a period of 30 minutes.

Although milk and beer are the products most commonly pasteurized, the process is applied to a few other foods as well. For example, canned apple juice is frequently pasteurized to kill bacteria that might cause the juice to ferment. (See also *Milk.*)

PASTRAMI *(puh strä′ mē)*—A spicy beef product of Romanian origin now most commonly associated with the Jewish cuisine. Pastrami is prepared from meat taken from either the shoulder section or the plate (the leanest section just below the ribs) of a beef animal and then cured, spiced, and smoked in that order. Pastrami resembles corned beef in outward appearance, but it has more spiciness.

Pastrami is delectable served either hot or cold. It is most desirable when predominantly lean, particularly when it is served as a hot dish. Cold pastrami and dark bread generously spread with prepared mustard make a delicious combination.

PASTRY—1. An unleavened dough made primarily of flour, water, and shortening. This type of pastry, prepared from basic ingredients or from a packaged piecrust mix, is used as a crust for pies and tarts. Good pastry is tender yet not crumbly, flaky, and golden brown. 2. A general name for many types of sweet baked goods. For example, tarts, cream puffs, and sweet rolls are called pastries.

Pastry has very few ingredients—flour, water, shortening, and salt—but each ingredient is very important. As with breads, cakes, and other baked goods, it is the gluten (an elastic protein) in the flour that forms the structure of pastry. Gluten is formed when the flour is moistened. Liquids such as milk can be used, but water is most commonly employed because it produces an easy-to-handle pastry. The fat in pastry tenderizes it by shortening the gluten strands. Fat also adds richness and flavor. The salt in pastry is for flavor only.

The homemaker who can make tender, flaky pastry is greatly admired. Although some cooks may claim to have a secret, you'll find that with a little practice you, too, can make excellent pastry.

Even though only a few ingredients are needed to make pastry, the way in which they are combined and the manner in which the pastry is handled are very important in making good pastry. First, measure all pastry ingredients accurately, using standard measuring cups and spoons. Then, follow the recipe instructions carefully. Remember two things in particular: (**1**) don't add more or less of an ingredient than is specified since this will throw off balance; and (**2**) don't overmix.

Although there are several methods of mixing pastry, the most common technique involves combining the fat and the flour, then mixing in the water. For this method, first cut the shortening into the flour (using a chopping motion) with a pastry blender or fork until the mixture is like coarse meal. For an extra-tender pastry, cut in half of the shortening until the mixture looks like cornmeal, then cut in the remaining shortening until the lumps in the mixture are the size of small peas. Flakiness in pastry is the result of fat-flour layers which separate during baking by steam. The way you combine fat, flour, and water determines this layering.

After the fat and flour are combined, sprinkle the water, a few drops at a time, over the flour mixture and toss the mixture lightly with a fork. As soon as part of the flour is moistened, push it aside and repeat with more of the flour mixture. (Don't stir the water into the flour mixture since this develops the gluten, which tends to make the pastry tough and rubbery.) It's not necessary to moisten every last particle of flour because it will all be moist enough when you push the dough gently into a ball. Be careful not to knead the dough or push it hard, as this also makes dough tough by overdeveloping the gluten.

Fluted edge: Trim pastry ½ inch beyond rim; fold under. Indent pastry, using knife handle wedged between thumb and index finger.

Spiral edge: Moisten rim of pastry; press end of ¾-inch pastry strip in place. Twist strip to form spiral; press in place.

Zigzag edge: Trim pastry ½ to 1 inch beyond pie plate edge; fold under. Press dough at slant between thumb and bent index finger.

Crisscross edge: Moisten pastry rim. Loosely interlace two ½-inch wide pastry strips; secure by pressing bottom strip against rim.

Scalloped edge: Trim pastry ½ inch beyond rim; fold under. Using measuring spoon, press dough against thumb and finger.

Fancy Scallop: Trim pastry ½ inch beyond rim; pinch together. Cut design with teaspoon; mark with fork. Brush with milk.

Twisted lattice: Using ¾-inch wide strips of pastry, twist and lay on pie filling. Weave diagonally with twisted cross strips.

Zigzag lattice: Cut strips with pastry wheel for pretty edge. Weave. Seal crust over lattice ends; make design with teaspoon.

Fluted edge: Seal in juices by folding rim of lower crust over ends of lattice strips. Press with fingers as shown for pretty edge.

Leaf trim: For leaves, bend doughnut "hole" cutter into leaf shape; then cut pastry. Overlap leaves around rim; press in place.

Spiral top: Make long ¾-inch wide pastry strip by pressing together shorter strips. Twist and form spiral atop pie as shown.

Decorative meringue: Pipe rows of meringue atop pie, using a pastry tube. Crisscross with four more rows. Brown as directed.

<table>
<tr><td>

Common pastry problems

Tough
    Not enough fat
    Too much water
    Overmixing
    Too much flour added when rolling out

Crumbly
    Not enough water
    Too much fat

Does not brown
    Rolled too thick
    Underbaked
    Overmixed

Shrinks
    Stretched when put in pan
    Overhandled
    Rolled too thin

Large blisters
    Not pricked enough
    Baked at too low a temperature

</td></tr>
</table>

Once the pastry is mixed, it must be rolled out to the desired shape. Roll the dough on a lightly floured board or pastry cloth, using a rolling pin. Flatten the ball of dough slightly with gentle pressure, making sure there are no ragged edges. For perfect pastry circles, press dough with the edge of your hand three times in both directions. Then roll the dough to ⅛-inch thickness, rolling from center to edge of dough with light strokes. Lift the rolling pin at the edge of dough to avoid stretching. Don't lift dough to turn it over or reposition it. For oil pastry, follow directions for rolling dough between sheets of waxed paper.

To transfer rolled dough to the pie plate, fold the dough in half and place the fold across the center of the plate, or roll it up on the rolling pin and unroll it over the plate. Be sure to ease the pastry into the plate; stretching the dough causes it to shrink during baking.

Bake the pastry, either unfilled or filled, as directed in the recipe.

Plain Pastry

For one single-crust pie or 4 to 6 tart shells—

  1½ **cups sifted all-purpose flour**
   ½ **teaspoon salt**
   ½ **cup shortening**
   4 **to 5 tablespoons cold water**

For one 8-, 9-, or 10-inch double-crust or lattice-top pie; two 8-, 9-, or 10-inch single-crust pies; or 6 to 8 tart shells—

  2 **cups sifted all-purpose flour**
  1 **teaspoon salt**
  ⅔ **cup shortening**
  5 **to 7 tablespoons cold water**

In mixing bowl sift flour and salt together; cut in shortening with pastry blender till pieces are the size of small peas. (For extra tender pastry, cut in *half* the shortening till like cornmeal. Cut in remaining till like small peas.) Sprinkle 1 tablespoon water over part of mixture. Gently toss with fork; push to side of bowl. Repeat till all is moistened.

Form into a ball. (For double-crust and lattice-top pies, divide dough for lower and upper crust and form into balls.) Flatten on lightly floured surface by pressing with edge of hand 3 times across in both directions. Roll from center to edge till ⅛ inch thick.

To bake single-crust pie shells: Fit pastry into pie plate; trim ½ to 1 inch beyond edge. Fold under and flute edge by pressing dough with forefinger against wedge made of finger and thumb of other hand. Prick bottom and sides well with fork. (If filling and crust are baked together, *do not prick.*) Bake at 450° till golden, about 10 to 12 minutes.

For lattice-top pie: Trim lower crust ½ inch beyond edge of pie plate. Roll remaining dough ⅛ inch thick. Cut strips of pastry ½ to ¾ inch wide with pastry wheel or knife. Lay strips on filled pie at 1-inch intervals. Fold back alternate strips as you weave cross strips. Trim lattice even with outer rim of pie plate; fold lower crust over strips. Seal; flute edge.

For double-crust pie: Trim lower crust even with rim of pie plate. Cut slits in top crust. Lift pastry by rolling it over rolling pin; then unroll loosely over well-filled pie. Trim ½ inch beyond edge. Tuck top crust under edge of lower crust. Flute edge of pastry, if desired.

Electric Mixer Pastry

Measure ¼ cup cold water, ½ cup shortening, 1¼ cups instant-type flour, and ½ teaspoon salt into small mixer bowl. Mix at lowest speed on electric mixer till dough begins to form, 15 to 30 seconds. Shape into ball. Roll and finish as directed in Plain Pastry. Makes one 8- or 9-inch single-crust pie.

Oil Pastry

Sift together 2 cups sifted all-purpose flour, and 1½ teaspoons salt. Pour ½ cup salad oil and 5 tablespoons cold water into measuring cup (*do not stir*). Add all at once to flour mixture. Stir lightly with fork. Form dough into 2 balls; flatten dough slightly.

Between two 12-inch squares waxed paper, roll dough in circle to edge of paper. (First dampen table to prevent slipping.) Peel off top paper and fit dough, paper side up, into pie plate. Remove paper. Finish as in Plain Pastry. Makes one 8- or 9-inch double-crust pie.

Egg Pastry

Sift together 4 cups sifted all-purpose flour, 1 tablespoon sugar, and 2 teaspoons salt. Cut in 1½ cups shortening. Combine 1 beaten egg, 1 tablespoon vinegar, and ½ cup cold water; sprinkle over flour-shortening mixture, 1 tablespoon at a time. Gently toss with fork; push to side of bowl. Repeat till all is moistened. Store in refrigerator in tightly covered container. Makes four 9-inch pastry shells.

Rich Tart Shell

Stir ½ cup butter to soften; blend in ¼ cup sugar and ¼ teaspoon salt. Add 1 egg; mix well. Stir in 1½ cups sifted all-purpose flour. Chill slightly. On floured surface, roll out to 12-inch circle. Using rolling pin to transfer dough, carefully place over outside of 9-inch round cake pan or fit into flan pan. (Shape dough to sides of pan *almost* to rim. Be sure there are *no thin places* in pastry.) Trim.

Place pan, crust up, on baking sheet. Bake at 450° till lightly browned, 8 to 10 minutes. Cool slightly; transfer to serving plate.

PASTRY BAG—A utensil consisting of a cone-shaped, flexible bag with a decorative tip at the point of the cone. Soft doughs and frostings are formed into fancy shapes by forcing them through the tip.

PASTRY BLENDER—A utensil consisting of several heavy wires or narrow metal strips bent into a U-shape and attached to a handle. A pastry blender is used to cut shortening into flour when making pastry.

PASTRY BRUSH—A soft-bristled brush used to apply glazes such as melted butter, beaten egg whites, and milk to baked goods, particularly pies or breads.

PASTRY CLOTH—A piece of heavy fabric on which pastry is rolled out. Since pastry dough does not stick to the floured cloth, a pastry cloth is favored over many other surfaces for rolling out dough.

PASTY (*pas′ tē*)—The British word for a pie or turnover filled with a meat-vegetable mixture. (See also *English Cookery*.)

PÂTÉ (*pä tā′*)—1. The French word for a pie filled with meat or fish. 2. A spreadable mixture of meat and seasonings served as an appetizer. The meat used for pâtés is so finely chopped or mashed that the mixture is the consistency of paste.

Tuna Pâté

1 8-ounce package cream cheese, softened
2 tablespoons chili sauce
2 tablespoons snipped parsley
1 teaspoon instant minced onion
½ teaspoon bottled hot pepper sauce
. . .
2 6½- or 7-ounce cans tuna, drained
Assorted crackers

Blend cream cheese, chili sauce, parsley, onion, and hot pepper sauce; gradually stir in tuna. Beat till well blended. Pack in a 4-cup mold or small bowl; chill thoroughly, at least 3 hours. At serving time, unmold on serving plate. Serve with crackers. Makes 3 cups.

Corned Beef Pâté

Made quickly with the electric blender—

Soften 2 teaspoons instant minced onion in ⅔ cup water for 5 minutes. Flake one 12-ounce can corned beef with fork; add 8 ounces braunschweiger, ½ cup mayonnaise or salad dressing, 1 tablespoon vinegar, ½ teaspoon dry mustard, and the onion mixture.

Place about ½ cup mixture in blender container; cover and blend at medium speed till smooth. Remove from blender. Repeat with remaining mixture. Turn into 3½-cup mold or bowl; chill. Unmold onto serving plate. Serve with crackers, rye bread rounds, or crisp rye wafers. Makes about 3¼ cups.

Ham Pâté

    1 beaten egg
  ¼ cup milk
  ¼ cup finely chopped onion
    2 tablespoons catsup
    4 teaspoons prepared mustard
    4 to 5 drops bottled hot pepper
        sauce
1½ cups ground fully cooked ham
    Assorted crackers

Combine first 6 ingredients; add ham and mix well. Pack into greased 5½x3x2¼-inch loaf pan. Bake at 325° for 1 hour. Cool, then unmold onto serving plate. Chill. Serve cold with assorted crackers. Makes 1¾ cups.

Begin a buffet by serving Tuna Pâté with assorted crackers as the appetizer. Canned tuna is combined with a peppy cream cheese mixture in this delicious, yet unusual pâté.

Chicken Liver Pâté

1 pound fresh or frozen chicken
    livers, thawed
Butter or margarine
3 tablespoons mayonnaise
2 tablespoons lemon juice
2 tablespoons butter, softened
1 tablespoon finely chopped onion
8 to 10 drops bottled hot pepper
    sauce
½ teaspoon salt
½ teaspoon dry mustard
Dash pepper
Chopped hard-cooked egg, snipped
    chives, *or* snipped parsley
Assorted crackers

Cook chicken livers, covered, in small amount of butter or margarine, stirring occasionally, till no longer pink. Put cooked livers through a meat grinder; blend with remaining ingredients. Place mixture in a 2-cup mold. Chill several hours; carefully unmold. Garnish with chopped hard-cooked egg, snipped chives, or snipped parsley. Serve with crackers.

Braunschweiger Pâté

1 pound braunschweiger
2 packages green onion dip mix
1 teaspoon sugar
2 teaspoons water
1 tablespoon garlic spread
2 3-ounce packages cream cheese,
    softened
1 tablespoon milk
⅛ teaspoon bottled hot pepper
    sauce
Snipped parsley
Radish slices
Crackers or melba toast

Mash braunschweiger. Combine green onion dip mix, sugar, and water. Add to braunschweiger; blend thoroughly. Form mixture into an igloo shape; place on serving plate. Chill thoroughly. Melt garlic spread. Whip softened cream cheese with milk and hot pepper sauce. Blend in melted garlic spread. Spread cream cheese mixture over braunschweiger; chill. Before serving, garnish with snipped parsley and radish slices; serve with crackers or melba toast.

Brandied Pâté Ring

1 8-ounce package frozen chicken
    livers, thawed and drained
¼ cup chopped onion
¼ cup finely chopped celery
¼ cup butter or margarine
¾ cup chicken broth
¼ teaspoon paprika
¼ teaspoon salt
Dash pepper
½ clove garlic, minced
2 tablespoons brandy
1½ teaspoons unflavored gelatin
2 hard-cooked eggs
Assorted crackers

In medium skillet cook chicken livers, onion, and celery in butter or margarine till livers are browned and vegetables are tender. Add ¼ *cup* of the chicken broth, paprika, salt, pepper, and garlic. Simmer, covered, about 5 minutes; remove from heat and stir in brandy.

In small saucepan soften unflavored gelatin in remaining chicken broth. Heat to dissolve; set aside. Place chicken liver mixture in blender container; cover and blend at medium speed till smooth. Transfer to bowl and stir in gelatin. Chop 1 hard-cooked egg and egg white from second egg (reserve remaining yolk). Add chopped egg to liver mixture. Chill till partially set; turn into a 3-cup mold. Refrigerate several hours or overnight. Unmold onto serving plate. (If desired, stir 1 teaspoon prepared mustard into ½ cup mayonnaise; spread on mold.) Sieve the reserved egg yolk over top. Serve with crackers.

PÂTÉ A CHOU (*pä ta shoo'*)—The French name for cream puffs or other puff pastry.

PÂTÉ DE FOIE GRAS (*pä tä' duh fwä' grä'*) —A French delicacy made of fattened goose livers mashed to form a paste. In many *pâté de foie gras* recipes, truffles, butter, mushrooms, and seasonings are used to complement the goose liver flavor.

This gourmet dish was first concocted in France during the eighteenth century. At first, it was restricted to the tables of high government officials, but after the French Revolution, the special recipe became more widely known. Frenchmen have handed down *pâté de foie gras* recipes from generation to generation. Even today, the world's rather limited supply of this gourmet food comes from France where it is prepared from secret recipes.

The most important ingredient in this delicious pâté is the goose livers. However, they must have an unnaturally high fat content. In order to get goose livers of this kind, the geese are confined in pens and force-fed several times a day. After about a month of this feeding, the goose's liver weighs about a pound and is ready for use in *pâté de foie gras*.

PATTY—A small, flat, circular mass of food. Meats, especially ground beef, vegetables, and candies are the foods most commonly made into patties.

PATTYPAN SQUASH—A summer squash also called cymling or scallop squash. This disc-shaped vegetable is characterized by a fluted edge. The most common variety has a light green to white exterior, depending on its maturity, and a green interior. There is also a yellow-skinned version.

Like other summer squash, pattypan squash may be cut up, rind and all, and cooked briefly by boiling or frying. Another cooking method is to halve the squash and bake it with stuffing or seasonings. Light seasonings such as salt, pepper, butter, brown sugar or honey, and nutmeg are recommended. (See also *Squash*.)

PATTY SHELL—Puff pastry formed into a shallow-cup shape before baking. Saucy main dishes are particularly good served in crisp patty shells.

Black Magic Luncheon

Cook 3 cups diced fully cooked ham and ½ cup chopped onion in 2 tablespoons butter or margarine till onion is tender but not brown. Remove from heat. Blend together 2 tablespoons all-purpose flour and ⅔ cup milk; stir into 2 cups dairy sour cream. Add sour cream mixture to meat with ½ cup sliced ripe olives.

Heat through, stirring constantly; *do not boil*. Stir in ¼ cup toasted slivered almonds. Serve in baked patty shells. Makes 8 servings.

Shrimp Thermidor

Equally delicious with tuna or crab, too—

    ¼ cup chopped onion
    2 tablespoons chopped green pepper
    2 tablespoons butter or margarine
        • • •
    1 10¼-ounce can frozen condensed
        cream of potato soup
    ¾ cup light cream
    ½ cup shredded sharp process
        American cheese
    2 teaspoons lemon juice
    1½ cups cooked or canned shrimp,
        split lengthwise
    Patty shells, baked

Cook onion and green pepper in butter or margarine till they are tender but not brown. Add soup and cream; heat slowly, stirring constantly, till blended. Bring the mixture just to boiling. Add shredded cheese to the mixture; stir to melt. Add lemon juice and shrimp. Heat through. Serve this dish in baked patty shells. Makes 4 to 5 servings.

Tangy Tuna

A very special fix-up for tuna—

    3 tablespoons butter or margarine
    3 tablespoons all-purpose flour
    ¾ cups milk
    ½ teaspoon Worcestershire sauce
    ¼ teaspoon salt
    ⅛ teaspoon pepper
    ⅓ cup grated Parmesan cheese
    1 6½- or 7-ounce can tuna, drained
    2 tablespoons chopped canned
        pimiento
    6 patty shells, baked

In saucepan melt butter or margarine. Stir in flour. Add milk, Worcestershire sauce, salt, and pepper. Cook over medium heat, stirring constantly, till mixture is thickened and bubbly. Cook 1 minute more. Stir in grated Parmesan Cheese. Cook over low heat till cheese melts, about 1 minute. Add drained tuna and chopped pimiento; heat through. Place hot patty shells on serving plates; generously spoon in tuna mixture. Makes 6 servings.

Shrimp Newburg

    8 frozen patty shells
    2 10-ounce cans frozen cream of
        shrimp soup
    1 cup milk
    2 cups cleaned, peeled, cooked
        shrimp
    1 16-ounce can peas, drained
    ¼ cup dry sherry
    1 4-ounce package shredded sharp
        natural Cheddar cheese

Bake patty shells according to package directions. In blazer pan of chafing dish, combine soup and milk; heat over direct heat. Add shrimp and peas. Continue heating, stirring constantly, till just simmering. Cook slowly about 5 to 10 minutes.

Stir in sherry and *half* the cheese. Sprinkle remaining cheese in patty shells. Spoon newburg into shells. Makes 8 servings.

PEA—A round, wrinkled or smooth seed of the legume family that is eaten as a vegetable. To most people, the fresh, green seeds are most common, but there are numerous other varieties available in dry or fresh form as well. All the members of this family, nonetheless, are descendants of the species *Pisum sativum*. In fact, the Latin word *pisum* was, over the years, changed to pease and finally to a more singular sounding word, pea.

Peas, preserved for centuries in dry form, have revealed much historical information concerning the eating habits of ancient peoples. Dry peas that are over 5,000 years old have been found in the remains of the Swiss "lake dwellers."

It has been fairly well established that there were three major areas of pea plant development—North Africa, the Near East, and central Asia. Although there is some question as to whether the Egyptians used

Fanciful cooking in a jiffy

←Classic Shrimp Newburg has been updated to get the hostess out of the kitchen. Convenience products save you much work.

them as food, peas have been found in many ancient Egyptian tombs. Field peas were eaten and possibly cultivated in the Near East about 6 or 7 B.C.

From all indications, the Indo-Iranian Aryans introduced peas to the early Greeks and Romans. Pea soup, much liked in Greece, was made and sold by street vendors. In Italy, peas were an important food to the lower classes. The Roman author Apicius devised many cooking methods for peas, including one named after himself.

Peas in the fresh or green state were not consumed until the Middle Ages. At that time, peas were cooked in their pods and were shelled while they were eaten. In some cases the pods were eaten, too. The English were responsible for the development of many pea varieties and brought some of them to America for propagation. But peas were still a delicacy in France in the seventeenth century.

How peas are produced: Peas develop in pods on vinelike plants that thrive only in cool weather. This necessitates early spring planting in the North and late fall to early spring sowings in the South.

How peas are harvested depends on what state—dry or fresh—they are to be used in. Dry peas, also called field peas, are mechanically harvested. The plants are allowed to dry. Then, the seeds are threshed out of the pods. On the other hand, most fresh or garden peas are extracted from the pods by machine right in the fields, although a small number of fresh peas are marketed in the pods. Idaho and Washington produce the largest number of commercially marketed dry peas. California, New York, and New Jersey produce most of the fresh peas.

Dry peas: Whole dry peas are quite closely allied to dry beans. The basic cooking principles that have been set forth for dry beans are, therefore, applicable to the whole peas as well.

Nutritional value—Because they have been dehydrated, dry peas are concentrated in caloric and nutritive content. A half cup of cooked dry peas contains about 145 calories. A substantial proportion of the calories are contributed by protein. For best protein utilization, the peas should be accompanied by some meat, cheese, or other dairy product. One serving also contributes an excellent amount of the B vitamin, thiamine, and a fair amount of iron, calcium, and phosphorus to the diet.

Types of dry peas—The two most important varieties of dry peas are distinguishable by color—green and yellow. Flavor differences are slight, enabling them to be used interchangeably in recipes. They may be processed as whole or split seeds. Split peas are prepared by removing the thin skins; a natural break in the skinned seeds causes the peas to split in half.

How to select and store—In most all supermarkets, dry peas are prepackaged in plastic bags or cardboard boxes to ensure the cleanliness of the product.

Dry peas, when stored tightly covered in a cool, dry place, can be held indefinitely. An opened package of dry peas should be placed in a well-sealed container.

How to prepare—Before soaking or cooking, rinse all dry peas in cold water. Like dry beans, whole dry peas require some soaking time to soften the outer skins. Split peas are soaked only when the shape of the peas is to be retained.

For each pound of whole dry peas being soaked, use 5⅔ cups of cold water. Soak the peas overnight or, for quicker results, bring the water to boiling. Add the peas and boil, covered, for 2 minutes. Remove from heat and soak the peas 1 hour.

If split peas are to retain their shape after cooking, boil 1 pound of peas in 4⅔ cups boiling water for 2 minutes. Remove the boiled peas from the heat and soak, covered, for about ½ hour.

To cook soaked whole peas, cover and simmer them till tender, about 1 hour. If the peas are to be used in a baked dish, cook them only till *almost* tender.

For a purée of split peas, no soaking is required. Simply use 4⅔ cups of cold water for each pound of peas being puréed. Bring the water to boiling, add the peas, then cover and simmer the peas for about 45 to 50 minutes.

How to use—Dry peas are best known for the delicious, thick soups that they produce. Spruce up the convenient canned or frozen pea soups when time is short.

Peas and Potato Soup

Combine one 12-ounce package frozen hashed brown potatoes, 4 cups water, 2 tablespoons instant minced onion, and 1 beef bouillon cube. Cover; cook till potatoes are tender. Stir in two 11¼-ounce cans condensed split pea-with-ham soup; add ½ teaspoon garlic powder and dash pepper. Simmer 5 minutes. Makes 4 servings.

Less frequently made but equally good are casseroles and baked vegetable dishes based on dry peas. Try pea stuffing in vibrant green peppers. Or flavor a split pea purée with ham, bacon, or onion.

Creamy Ham Towers

    6 frozen patty shells, baked
    1 11¼-ounce can condensed green
        pea soup
    2 cups cubed fully cooked ham
    ⅓ cup sliced pitted ripe olives
    2 tablespoons snipped parsley
    2 tablespoons chopped canned
        pimiento
    ½ cup dairy sour cream

Warm baked patty shells at 325° for 5 minutes. Meanwhile, blend together soup and ½ cup water; heat and stir till boiling. Stir in ham, olives, parsley, and pimiento; heat through.

Stir in sour cream; heat through (do not boil). Spoon into warm patty shells. Serves 6.

Fresh peas: Fresh varieties of peas, whether podded or not, are noted especially for their sweet flavor and their attractive emerald green color. Fresh peas are as nutritious as they are good-tasting.

Nutritional value—In each serving of fresh peas, there's a storehouse of nutrients. Two-thirds cup of cooked fresh peas

Extraordinary delicacy

Freshly shelled peas cook to unequaled →
sweet and delicate flavor when a dash of sugar is added to the cooking water.

contains about 70 calories. This same serving also provides an excellent supply of the B vitamins, thiamine and niacin, good amounts of vitamin C, iron, and the B vitamin, riboflavin, and some vitamin A.

Types of fresh peas—One method of classifying the more than 200 fresh or garden pea varieties is according to the skin appearance—wrinkled or smooth. Although the wrinkled varieties are generally higher in sugar content, many people still prefer the smooth-skinned peas because of their exceptionally good flavor.

One popular pea variety from the Orient is eaten pod and all. Known as sugar peas, snow peas, or Chinese pea pods, these peas are picked and used when the seeds are underdeveloped and the thin-skinned pea pods are still crisp and sweet.

How to select and store—Only a small portion of fresh peas are marketed in the pod. The majority are shelled in the field and within a few hours have been commercially canned or frozen. You can choose from a variety of these processed peas—plain or in seasonings such as butter, cream sauce, or vegetable mixtures.

If fresh peas are available, select those whose pods are bright green, well-filled, crisp, and velvety to the touch. Yellowing pods indicate overmature, tough seeds. Mildewed, excessively swelled, or speckled pods should be avoided, too.

As is the case with corn, fresh peas rapidly lose their sweetness after they have been picked. It is desirable, therefore, to use them as quickly as possible after harvesting. If the peas must be held for a brief period, refrigerate them, leaving the peas in their pods.

How to prepare—Fresh peas are easy to prepare. Simply shell the peas and wash them in cold water. Cover and cook in a small amount of boiling, salted water until crisp-tender, about 8 to 15 minutes, depending on the size of the peas.

How to use—Buttered peas is one of the more popular hot vegetable dishes. So are peas-and-potatoes and peas-and-onions, which are so often dressed with a creamy white sauce. For a change from the ordinary, add a seasoning such as chili powder, marjoram, mint, mustard, oregano, poppy seed, rosemary, sage, or savory.

One-Step Creamed Peas

    1 cup *cold* milk
    1 16-ounce can peas, drained
    ½ teaspoon instant minced onion
    2 tablespoons instant-type flour
    ½ teaspoon salt
    ¼ teaspoon pepper
    2 tablespoons butter or margarine

Pour milk over peas; stir in remaining ingredients. Cook and stir over medium heat till mixture comes to boiling; boil 1 minute. Makes about 4 servings.

Peas in Cream

    3 tablespoons butter or margarine
    ½ cup water
    1 to 1½ cups fresh shelled peas
        (1 to 1½ pounds in shell)
    2 cups finely torn leaf lettuce
    2 tablespoons finely chopped onion
    1 tablespoon snipped parsley
    1 teaspoon sugar
    ½ teaspoon salt
      Dash pepper
    ⅓ cup light cream

In saucepan heat butter and water to boiling. Add peas, lettuce, onion, parsley, sugar, salt, and pepper. Cover; simmer 8 to 15 minutes. Do not drain. Add cream. Makes 4 servings.

Springtime Peas

    2 pounds fresh peas, unshelled
    3 to 6 lettuce leaves
    ⅓ cup sliced green onion
            . . .
    1 teaspoon sugar
    ½ teaspoon salt
      Dash pepper
      Dash dried thyme leaves,
        crushed
    3 tablespoons butter or margarine

Shell peas. Cover bottom of skillet with lettuce; top with peas and onion. Sprinkle on sugar and seasonings; add butter. Cover tightly and cook over *low heat* till peas are done, 10 to 15 minutes. Makes 4 servings.

Oven Peas

In a 1½-quart casserole combine two 10-ounce packages frozen peas, thawed enough to separate the peas; one 3-ounce can sliced mushrooms, drained (½ cup); ¼ cup chopped onion; ¼ teaspoon salt; ¼ teaspoon dried savory leaves, crushed; dash pepper; 2 tablespoons butter; and 1 tablespoon water. Cover the mixture; bake at 350° till the peas are tender, about 1 hour. Stir once or twice. Makes 8 servings.

Epicurean Peas

    4 slices bacon, chopped
    1 tablespoon chopped onion
    1 cup fresh mushrooms, sliced,
        or 1 3-ounce can broiled sliced
        mushrooms, drained
    2 tablespoons butter or margarine
    1 tablespoon all-purpose flour
    1 cup light cream
      Salt and pepper
    1 16-ounce can peas, drained,
        or 1 10-ounce package frozen
        peas, cooked and drained
      Timbale Cases

In a skillet fry bacon till crisp; remove bacon from pan. Cook onion and fresh mushrooms in bacon fat till tender. Drain remaining fat. Melt butter in a saucepan and blend in flour. Add cream all at once. Cook quickly, stirring constantly, till mixture thickens.

Add salt and pepper to taste. Stir in peas and mushrooms. Add cooked bacon and heat through. Spoon hot mixture into Timbale Cases. If desired, top with additional crumbled bacon. Makes 6 servings.

Timbale Cases: Sift together 1 cup sifted all-purpose flour, 1 tablespoon sugar, and ¼ teaspoon salt. Add 1 cup milk to 2 well-beaten eggs. Stir in flour mixture; beat smooth.

Heat timbale iron in deep hot fat (375°) for 2 minutes. Drain excess fat from iron; dip into batter to within ¼ inch of top. Return at once to hot fat. Fry until case is crisp and golden brown and will slip from iron.

Turn the timbale case upside down to drain. Reheat iron 1 minute; make next timbale case. Repeat, using up batter. (If the batter slips off, the iron is too cold; if the batter sticks, the iron has been heated to too hot a temperature.)

Luxe Peas and Celery

    2 tablespoons butter or margarine
    ½ cup bias-cut celery slices
    1 3-ounce can broiled sliced
        mushrooms, drained
    2 tablespoons chopped canned
        pimiento
    2 tablespoons finely chopped onion
    ½ teaspoon salt
    ¼ teaspoon dried savory leaves,
        crushed
      Dash freshly ground pepper
    1 16-ounce can peas, drained,
        or 1 10-ounce package frozen
        peas, cooked and drained

Melt butter or margarine in skillet. Add celery, mushrooms, pimiento, onion, salt, savory, and pepper. Stirring frequently, cook mixture, uncovered, till celery is crisp-tender, about 5 minutes. Add peas to the mixture; heat the mixture just till hot. Makes 4 servings.

Smoky Peas and Potatoes

    1½ pounds small potatoes
     1 to 1½ pounds fresh peas
        (1 to 1½ cups shelled)
     2 tablespoons butter or margarine
     2 tablespoons all-purpose flour
    1⅔ cups milk
     1 6-ounce roll smoked process
        cheese
     4 slices, bacon, crisp-cooked,
        drained, and crumbled

Scrub potatoes; peel off narrow strip around center of each. Cook in boiling, salted water just till done, about 15 to 20 minutes; drain. Meanwhile, cook fresh peas in small amount of boiling, salted water till tender, about 8 to 15 minutes; drain thoroughly.

In small saucepan melt butter or margarine. Stir in flour; add milk all at once. Cook and stir till mixture is thickened and bubbly. Cut roll of cheese into small pieces; add to sauce. Cook and stir over low heat till the cheese melts. Add *half* of the crumbled bacon.

Combine hot potatoes and peas in serving dish; pour on a little cheese sauce. Sprinkle with remaining bacon. Serve immediately; pass remaining sauce. Makes 5 or 6 servings.

Quick Creole Peas

　1　10-ounce package frozen peas
　¼　cup chopped onion
　¼　cup chopped green pepper
　2　tablespoons butter or margarine
　　　　• • •
　1　8-ounce can tomatoes
　½　teaspoon salt
　　　Dash pepper
　1　tablespoon cornstarch

Cook peas according to package directions; drain. Cook onion and green pepper in butter till tender but not brown.

Reserve 2 tablespoons tomato liquid. Cut tomatoes in pieces and add to cooked onion. Stir in salt, pepper, and the drained peas. Heat mixture to boiling. Combine cornstarch with the reserved tomato liquid and stir them into peas. Cook and stir till the mixture thickens and bubbles. Makes 3 or 4 servings.

Peas go well in cold salads, too. Use them in tossed vegetable or main dish combinations, main dish salads, and shimmering salad molds. Canned peas are particularly suited for these salad recipes.

Herbed Pea Salad

　2　10-ounce packages frozen peas
　⅓　cup clear French salad dressing
　　　　with herbs and spices
　½　teaspoon dried dillweed
　1　cup thinly sliced celery
　1　hard-cooked egg, sliced

Cook peas according to package directions; drain. Combine salad dressing with dillweed; pour over peas and celery. Chill several hours or overnight, stirring occasionally. Serve in lettuce-lined bowl, if desired. Top salad with egg slices. Makes 6 to 8 servings.

A favorite, dressed up

← A smoke-flavored cheese sauce mingles with a matchless vegetable combo for Smoky Peas and Potatoes. Crumbled bacon dots top.

Colorful and flavorful peas greatly boost the appeal of soups, stews, and casseroles. Added to meat mixtures, they transform a main dish into a meal-in-one specialty. (See also *Vegetable*.)

Beef Oriental

Pour boiling water over one 7-ounce package frozen Chinese pea pods and carefully break apart with fork; drain immediately.

In skillet cook 1 pound lean ground beef in 1 tablespoon salad oil till beef is brown. Push beef to one side of skillet. Add ¼ cup chopped onion and 1 small clove garlic, minced; cook just for a few seconds. Add 4 cups thinly sliced raw cauliflowerets (1 medium head) and 1 cup canned condensed beef broth. Stirring gently, cook the mixture till the cauliflower is crisp-tender, about 3 minutes.

Mix together 2 tablespoons cornstarch, ½ teaspoon monosodium glutamate, ½ cup cold water, and ¼ cup soy sauce till blended. Stir into mixture in skillet. Add the pea pods. Cook, stirring constantly, till sauce thickens and bubbles. Serve with hot cooked rice. Pass additional soy sauce, if desired. Serves 6.

Stack-a-Dinner

In skillet brown 1 pound ground beef with ½ cup chopped onion. Drain off fat. Add one 8-ounce can tomato sauce with mushrooms; ¼ cup catsup; ¼ cup water; ½ teaspoon dried oregano leaves, crushed; 3 drops bottled hot pepper sauce; ¼ teaspoon salt; and dash pepper. Bring to boiling, stirring often.

Cook 2 cups uncooked packaged precooked rice and prepare one 10-ounce package frozen peas following package directions. On 6 individual serving plates layer rice, peas, and meat mixture. Sprinkle about a sixth of 4 ounces sharp process American cheese, shredded (1 cup), over each serving. Trim with sliced pimiento-stuffed green olives. Makes 6 servings.

PEA BEAN—A small, white kidney bean that is harvested when mature, then dried for food. When the bean has a black spot on its surface, it's called a black-eyed pea or a cowpea. (See also *Black-Eyed Pea*.)

PEACH

*Complete purchasing, storing, and serving
information on this delicate fruit of gold.*

Golden fruit, queen of fruit, Persian apples—these long-used nicknames for peaches are but one indication of how highly people throughout the centuries have regarded these fuzzy-skinned fruits. Equally complimentary are an assortment of symbolic phrases and beliefs referring to peaches. In the United States it is common to hear someone say, "her complexion is like peaches and cream," or "he's a peach of a person." In China peaches stand for immortality, and in Japan peach blossoms are a symbol of fertility.

In America, only apples and oranges are more popular than these sweet, juicy stone fruits. Called *Prunus persica* (Persian plums) by botanists, peaches are related to cherries, apricots, plums, and almonds. Although the origin of peaches is still disputed, many people believe that they may have descended from the wild almond.

The centuries-old belief that peaches originated in Persia has more recently been refuted. Early Chinese writers mention small, sour peaches that were growing wild in China 500 years before any Mideastern recorders refer to the existence of peaches in Persia. Peaches presumably were exported from China to Persia by traders in the pre-Christian Era.

This confusion probably occurred because people, such as Greeks and Romans, who traveled to Persia saw peaches for the first time and assumed that peaches originated there. For example, Greek soldiers first saw peaches around 300 B.C. in Persia when they were there on an army expedition headed by Alexander the Great. Shortly thereafter, Theophrastus, a Greek writer, labeled peaches "Persian fruit," a name these fruits have retained since.

Traders probably brought cuttings of the peach trees to Rome. Virgil, the first Roman writer to mention peaches, clearly indicates that there were some peach cultivating problems in Italy. Nevertheless, the Romans must have had a certain amount of success with peach cultivation, or peaches would not have spread to other regions of Europe as rapidly as they did.

France and Spain soon developed new peach varieties, and other types spread to England, Belgium, Holland, and Germany. Spanish explorers introduced peaches to the Western Hemisphere, making plantings in Mexico and Central America during the 1500s. In turn, the American Indian learned to cultivate peaches, and they spread their growth as far north as Pennsylvania and in inland territories, too, by the time Jamestown, Virginia, was settled by the English. A little later, the English in Massachusetts and the French in Louisiana brought peach varieties from their homelands and made plantings in their respective American settlements.

The development of United States commercial peach orchards was waylaid until the mid-1800s. America's first peach orchard venture was undertaken in Georgia, but poor seedlings were used as rootstocks. After 1850, better ways of cultivating peaches were developed, allowing orchard production to expand greatly. Today, the large production centers extend from coast to coast and include California, the East Coast states from Georgia to Massachusetts, Colorado, and Washington.

Fresh peaches deluxe

← Save room for dessert when Peach-Orange Shortcake, generously layered with whipped cream and sliced peaches, is to be served.

How peaches are produced: Making good-quality peaches available to homemakers entails many involved stages of production. The best peach varieties are not perpetuated by planting peach stones but rather by a special technique known as budding —inserting a bud of the desired tree into a seedling peach tree. This propagation technique is necessary because a peach stone does not produce exactly the same kind of tree from which it came. In addition, since peach trees are short-lived compared to many other fruit trees, peach orchards must be replanted more frequently. The trees cannot tolerate severe cold weather, although they do thrive in a climate with mild winters.

Most peaches that are to be marketed fresh are hand-harvested by specially trained pickers who know how to prevent fruit damage during handling. The fruit is mechanically defuzzed, then sorted, graded, and packed. Peaches must be marketed quickly, as they do not keep well.

Nutritional value: Amazing as it may seem, tree-borne peaches are almost 90 percent water; thus, they are relatively low in calories. One medium raw peach contains

Fuzzy-skinned peaches in the foreground and smooth-skinned nectarines on right side of dish are similar in all other respects.

about 40 calories—fewer than an apple (70 calories) or a pear (100 calories) of comparable size. When peaches are processed in sugar syrups, however, the sweetening adds a considerable number of calories. Two peach halves with 2 tablespoons of heavy syrup contain about 80 calories, while ⅓ cup frozen, sliced peaches provides about 90 calories.

Peaches also supply an assortment of vitamins and minerals. Vitamin A, the most prevalent vitamin, is present in above-average levels. Other nutrients are found in lesser quantities.

Types of peaches

The peach family includes thousands of different varieties. Even as early as 1916, one pomologist listed over 2000 varieties of peaches in the United States. Most of the peaches now grown for commercial purposes began as chance seedlings that were planted in the United States. The Elberta peach, one of the most well-known varieties, came from a stone planted in 1870 near Marshallville, Georgia.

Hybridists continue to develop new varieties that will have special characteristics for desired purposes. One, for example, might ripen earlier than all present varieties. Another might respond better to canning conditions, while a third variety might have good freezing qualities.

Peaches are categorized by the color of the flesh—yellow or white—and by how the stone releases from the flesh—clingstone, semiclingstone, or freestone. Although the white varieties are equally good, yellow-fleshed peaches are preferred in the United States. In Europe the use of white peaches predominates.

Clingstone and freestone are terms that clearly define the relationship of peach flesh to stone. Clingstone peaches have stones that adhere firmly to the flesh. These varieties are used primarily for canning. Freestones are the most popular type of peach for eating fresh since the meat releases readily from the stone. A few intermediate peaches known as semiclings are also available. In most cases, clings and semiclings mature earlier in the season than do freestones.

One unique variation of the peach is the smooth-skinned nectarine. In all other respects of fruit appearance, parent tree, and fruit blossoms, peaches and nectarines seem to be identical. Although it is not known where the event occurred, nectarines developed as an accidental peach mutation hundreds of years ago and, contrary to popular belief, are not a crossing between the peach and the plum.

How to select

Fresh peaches are available only from May through September, but they can be purchased in many processed forms during the rest of the year. Unlike some fruit, fresh peaches are not sold in retail outlets by grade; therefore, they must be judged by appearance and feel. On the other hand, processed peaches may be graded.

Fresh peaches: The most important point to remember when selecting fresh peaches is that the fruits do not continue to ripen after they have been picked. Peaches that were picked when immature may soften slightly and become more juicy, but they will still retain a green, unripe flavor.

Look for round, plump peaches that have a soft, creamy to yellow background color, that are devoid of brown spots or decay, and that are moderately firm or only slightly soft to the touch. Peaches that are tinged with green are immature and will shrivel rather than ripen. Those that are very soft to the touch are overripe. The amount of red blush on the skin is not an indication of ripeness but rather is determined by the variety.

Because peaches are quite perishable, wise shopping is imperative for maximum satisfaction. During July and August, the height of the peach-growing season, both price and quality are often at their best, but be sure to buy only what you can use. If home-grown peaches are available in your locality, consider buying quantities of peaches to can or freeze.

Frozen peaches: Frozen peaches, usually sliced freestones, are packed in a syrup or sugar combined with a color keeper such as ascorbic acid. Although not mandatory, United States government grades ranging from U.S. Grade A (Fancy) to U.S. Grade B (Choice) and U.S. Grade C (Standard) may appear on the label. The better the quality and uniformity of the fruit, the higher the grade. Select packages that are solidly frozen and show no signs of thawing or refreezing such as juice-stained boxes.

Canned peaches: Canned peaches are available as clingstones or freestones; whole, sliced, or halved; packed in syrup or water; and sweetened, spiced, or pickled. USDA grading of canned peaches, also voluntary, is a good guide to quality when available. Although the quality standards used to determine grades vary, the ratings used for canned peaches are the same as those used for frozen peaches.

Syrup classifications are determined by the percentage content of sugar. Common concentrations are extra heavy, heavy, light, and water-pack. The kind of liquid or syrup used is in no way connected to the quality of the fruit.

Another canned product, peach nectar, is a blend of extracted peach juice and a light sugar syrup. Peach nectar can be used as the basis for a beverage or as a recipe ingredient in entrées, side dishes, and a variety of desserts.

Dried peaches: Both clingstone and freestone peaches are available in dried form. The number and types of defects determine the grade of the product: U.S. Grade A (Fancy), U.S. Grade B (Choice), U.S. Grade C (Standard), or U.S. Grade D (Substandard). Most dried peaches are treated with sulfur dioxide to preserve the flavor and color of the fruit. The addition of this ingredient to the dried peaches must be indicated on the package label.

How many fresh peaches to buy

In general, one pound of peaches as purchased is equivalent to 3 medium peaches and will yield 2 cups sliced peaches or 1 cup peach pulp. For every pint of home-frozen or home-canned peaches, plan to buy 1 to 1½ pounds.

How to store

Because fresh peaches bruise easily, they must be handled very gently. Separate fully ripe peaches and refrigerate uncovered. Fully ripe peaches will keep in the refrigerator for three to five days. Allow the unripe fruit to mellow a few days at room temperature; then refrigerate.

The length of time that processed peaches can be stored is determined by the preservation method used. Store frozen peaches at 0° or less. They should be served within one year. Shelf-stable canned peaches also can be stored for up to one year. On the other hand, unopened packages of dried peaches keep for six to eight months. Once opened, store dried peaches in a tightly covered container. In hot, humid weather, peaches should be stored under refrigerated conditions.

How to use

Peaches are a popular family fruit because they taste so good in so many ways. They're delicious as a snack fruit, served atop hot or cold breakfast cereal, sweetened with sugar, or combined with cream. Equally good are accompaniments, salads, main dishes, and desserts that feature peaches.

As an accompaniment: Peach accompaniments can be both tasteful menu additions and artistic garnishes. Set off the meat entrée with pickled or spiced peaches. Fill broiled peaches with currant jelly as a companion to beef, poultry, and ham; or with mint jelly for lamb.

Spiced Peaches

    1 29-ounce can peach halves
    1 tablespoon mixed pickling
        spices *or* 3 to 6 inches stick
        cinnamon
    1 teaspoon whole cloves
    1 tablespoon vinegar

Combine all ingredients; heat to boiling. Reduce heat; simmer 5 minutes. Drain before serving. Stud with whole cloves, if desired. Serve warm or chilled.

Peach pointers

Peeling: Dip the peach in boiling water for a few seconds or twirl it over a hot flame. Use a knife to remove peel from the fruit.

Halving: Cut the peach in half through stem and blossom ends. Cup peach in palms of hands. Gently twist and pull the halves apart.

Keeping fresh-cut fruit bright: Immerse the cut peach pieces in sugar syrup; brush pieces with lemon, orange, or pineapple juice mixed with a little water; or use ascorbic acid color keeper as directed on the label.

Orange-Spiced Peaches

Drain one 29-ounce can peach halves, reserving ½ cup syrup. Tie ½ teaspoon whole cloves, 6 inches stick cinnamon, and 10 whole allspice in piece of cheesecloth. In saucepan combine reserved peach syrup; ⅓ cup vinegar; ½ cup sugar; ½ unpeeled orange, quartered and sliced; peaches; and bag of spices. Heat to boiling; simmer, covered, for about 5 minutes.

Let cool at room temperature. Remove spice bag. Serve warm or chilled; stud peaches with a few whole cloves, if desired. Serves 6 to 8.

Peach-Cantaloupe Conserve

In large kettle mix 3 cups chopped cantaloupe and 3 cups chopped peaches. Bring to a full rolling boil, stirring constantly. Add 4½ cups sugar and 3 tablespoons lemon juice; return to a full rolling boil. Boil 12 minutes. Add ½ teaspoon ground nutmeg, ¼ teaspoon salt, ¼ teaspoon grated orange peel, and ⅓ cup slivered blanched almonds; boil to jellying stage,* 4 to 5 minutes more. Pour into hot, scalded jars; seal at once. Makes about 3½ pints.

*Dip a large metal spoon in boiling mixture; remove and tilt spoon till syrup runs over side. When jellying stage is reached, liquid will stop flowing in a stream and divide in 2 distinct drops that run together and sheet from the edge of the spoon. On a thermometer, temperature should register 220° or 8 degrees higher than the boiling point in your locality.

In a salad: Peaches give side dish and main dish salads vibrant color and mouth-watering flavor. They can be as simple as the ever-popular peaches and cottage cheese combo or as ornate as carefully arranged peaches in a special gelatin mold.

Applesauce-Peach Salad

    1 3-ounce package lemon-flavored
         gelatin
    1 cup applesauce
    ½ cup chopped pecans
    1 large fresh peach, peeled and sliced,
         or 1 12-ounce package frozen
         sliced peaches*

Dissolve gelatin in 1½ cups boiling water. Chill till partially set. Stir in remaining ingredients. Turn into an 8x8x2-inch dish; chill till mixture is firm. Makes 6 servings.

  *If using frozen peaches, thaw and drain, reserving ½ cup syrup. *Dissolve gelatin in 1 cup boiling water instead of 1½ cups;* add reserved peach syrup. Continue as above.

Spiced Peach Mold

    1 8½-ounce can pineapple slices
    1 29-ounce jar spiced peaches
    2 3-ounce packages orange-
         pineapple-flavored gelatin
    2 tablespoons lemon juice
    ¼ teaspoon salt
    2 7-ounce bottles ginger ale,
         chilled (about 2 cups)

Drain and halve pineapple slices. Drain peaches, reserving syrup. Remove pits. Add water to syrup to make 2 cups. In a saucepan combine peach syrup mixture and gelatin; heat and stir till gelatin dissolves. Add lemon juice and salt. Chill till cold but not set.

  Pour ginger ale into gelatin; stir. Pour *half* the gelatin into 6½-cup ring mold; chill portions of gelatin till partially set.

  Arrange *most* of the peaches and pineapple around mold, gently placing fruit in the gelatin. Chill till *almost* firm. Cut any remaining peaches and pineapple and fold into reserved gelatin. Pour carefully over gelatin in mold. Chill till firm. Serves 8 to 10.

Peach-Cherry Sparkle

    1 16-ounce can pitted dark
         sweet cherries
    ½ cup sugar
    2 envelopes unflavored gelatin
         (2 tablespoons)
    ½ teaspoon salt
    ½ cup lemon juice
    2 7-ounce bottles ginger ale
         (about 2 cups)
    1 16-ounce can sliced peaches,
         drained and diced (1¼ cups)

Drain cherries, reserving syrup; add water to syrup to make 1¼ cups. In saucepan combine sugar, gelatin, and salt; stir in syrup. Cook and stir over medium heat till gelatin dissolves. Remove from heat; add lemon juice.

  Allow to cool but not set. Resting bottle on rim of pan, gradually pour in ginger ale, stirring gently with up-and-down motion. Chill till partially set. Fold in cherries and peaches. Turn into 6½-cup ring mold. Chill the mixture till firm. Makes 8 to 10 servings.

Berry-Peach Marble

    1 3-ounce package strawberry-
         flavored gelatin
    2 cups sliced fresh strawberries
    1 16-ounce can peach slices
    1 envelope unflavored gelatin
    2 tablespoons lemon juice
    1 2-ounce package dessert topping
         mix
    2 3-ounce packages cream cheese,
         softened

Dissolve strawberry-flavored gelatin in 1 cup boiling water; stir in 1 cup cold water. Chill till partially set. Fold in strawberries.

  Drain peaches, reserving syrup. Dice peaches. Add enough water to syrup to make 1 cup. Soften unflavored gelatin in syrup mixture; heat and stir till gelatin is dissolved. Stir in lemon juice. Cool. Prepare topping mix, following package directions; beat in cream cheese. Fold in peach-gelatin mixture and peaches. Chill till partially set.

  Layer strawberry- and cheese-gelatin mixtures in 7½-cup mold. Swirl knife through gently to marble. Chill till firm. Makes 10 servings.

Peach and Chicken Cups

Herbs and garlic-flavored croutons are the novel flavor twists—

½ cup dairy sour cream
¼ cup mayonnaise or salad dressing
½ teaspoon dried thyme leaves, crushed
¼ teaspoon dried basil leaves, crushed
Dash sugar
Dash salt
Dash pepper

. . .

2 cups cubed cooked chicken
1 8¾-ounce can sliced peaches, drained and diced

. . .

½ cup garlic-flavored croutons
1 green pepper, sliced crosswise into 4 thick rings

In bowl combine sour cream, mayonnaise or salad dressing, thyme, basil, sugar, salt, and pepper. Add cubed cooked chicken and sliced peaches, reserving a few sliced peaches for garnish; toss to coat. Chill. Just before serving, fold croutons into salad. Spoon chicken mixture into green pepper rings and garnish with reserved peach slices. Makes 4 servings.

In main dishes: A fruit salad featuring peaches is undoubtedly the main dish that first comes to mind, but peaches in main dishes offer considerably more versatility. In cooked entrées they are a unique addition to poultry stuffing or a refreshing flavor partner to baked luncheon meat. Prepare sandwiches with chopped peaches in chicken or turkey salad filling. For a teen-agers' party, use well-drained peach halves as the decorative touch atop a hearty salad sandwich loaf.

A glistening touch

←Before baking subtly flavored Peach Pie, sprinkle the lattice-top crust with a little granulated sugar for added glamour.

Peachy Corned Beef

Place one 3-pound piece corned beef in heavy saucepan; add water to cover. Add 1 bay leaf. Cover and simmer till tender, 2½ to 3 hours. Cool meat in liquid; remove. Slice across grain.

Place overlapping slices in an 11¾x7½x1¾-inch baking dish. Drain one 29-ounce can peach halves, reserving ¼ cup syrup. Place peaches around meat. Combine reserved syrup with ¼ cup brown sugar, ¼ cup catsup, 2 tablespoons vinegar, and 2 teaspoons prepared mustard. Pour over meat and peaches. Bake at 350° for 1 hour, basting occasionally. Makes 6 servings.

Ginger-Peachy Casserole

Combine two 16-ounce cans pork and beans in tomato sauce; 8 gingersnaps, finely crushed (½ cup); ¼ cup catsup; 2 tablespoons light molasses; and ½ teaspoon salt. Place *half* the bean mixture in bottom of 2-quart casserole. Arrange one 16-ounce can sliced peaches over beans; top with remaining bean mixture.

Drain one 12-ounce can luncheon meat; cut in 6 slices. Place slices atop beans. Cover and bake at 325° for 45 minutes. Uncover and bake 15 minutes more. Makes 5 to 6 servings.

Peach-Ham Swisser

1 unsliced loaf French bread
Butter or margarine, softened
Leaf lettuce
6 slices boiled ham
4 slices process Swiss cheese
1 16-ounce can peach halves, well-drained
½ cup mayonnaise
2 tablespoons chili sauce
1 tablespoon pickle relish

Cut bread in half lengthwise; store top half for later use. Cut thin slice off bottom half to make it sit flat; spread inside with butter. Arrange lettuce and ham atop bread. Cut cheese in halves diagonally; arrange the cheese triangles and peaches over ham.

Blend together mayonnaise, chili sauce, and pickle relish; drizzle this mixture over salad loaf. Garnish salad loaf with sprigs of watercress, if desired. Makes 6 servings.

As a dessert: Start chilly desserts or steamy baked dishes with peaches as the foundation. Summer finales such as peach ice cream and peach shortcake are choice fare when prepared with fresh peaches. Peach tapioca is a refreshingly light dessert course, too. Baked all-time favorites—peach pies, cobblers, cakes, and puddings—can be served hot from the oven or pleasantly warm. (See also *Fruit*.)

Peaches and Cream Milk Shake

    1 cup sliced peaches
    ¼ cup milk
    1 pint peach ice cream
    ¾ cup milk

Place peaches and the ¼ cup milk in blender container. Cover and blend till smooth, about 10 seconds. Spoon in ice cream; cover and blend again till softened. Add remaining milk; mix till blended. Sweeten with a little sugar, if desired. Pour into tall glasses. Garnish each serving with additional peach slices, if desired. Makes 3 or 4 servings.

Peaches in Flame

    ½ cup sugar
    ½ cup port wine
    ½ cup tart cherry jelly
    ¼ teaspoon ground cinnamon
      Dash salt
    1 tablespoon lime juice
    1 29-ounce can peach halves,
      drained
    ¼ cup brandy, heated
    1 quart lemon ice cream

Combine sugar, port wine, cherry jelly, cinnamon, salt, and lime juice in a blazer pan of chafing dish. Heat and stir until smoothly blended. Add peach halves, cut side down, then prick rounded surfaces of the peaches with a fork. Simmer about 5 minutes, basting the peach halves frequently with sauce.

Add the ¼ cup heated brandy, set aflame, and toss gently with silver fork and spoon until the flame dies. To serve, spoon the peaches and sauce over individual servings of lemon ice cream. Makes about 8 servings.

Peach-Orange Shortcake

    2 cups sifted all-purpose flour
    2 tablespoons sugar
    3 teaspoons baking powder
    ½ teaspoon salt
    ½ cup butter or margarine
    ⅔ cup light cream
    1 beaten egg
    1 teaspoon shredded orange peel
          • • •
    1 cup whipping cream
    4 cups sliced fresh peaches,
      lightly sugared

Sift together dry ingredients; cut in butter or margarine till mixture is like coarse crumbs. Combine cream, egg, and peel; add all at once to dry ingredients, stirring just till moistened. Spread in a greased 8x8x2-inch baking pan. Bake at 450° for 15 to 18 minutes. Remove from pan; cool on rack for about 3 minutes.

Split cake into 2 layers; place bottom layer on serving plate. Whip cream; spread about *three-fourths* of the whipped cream on bottom cake layer. Then top with peaches, reserving about 12 slices for a garnish. Top with second cake layer, remaining whipped cream, and reserved peaches. Makes 6 servings.

Peach-Easy Shortcake

    1 package 1-layer-size yellow
      cake mix
    1 30-ounce can sliced peaches
    2 tablespoons cornstarch
          • • •
    2 tablespoons butter or margarine
      Dash ground nutmeg
    ½ cup whipping cream

Prepare cake mix, using package directions. Turn into greased and floured 9x1½-inch round pan. Bake at 350° for 20 to 25 minutes. Cool 10 minutes. Remove from pan; cool. Drain peaches, reserving 1½ cups syrup. In saucepan gradually stir reserved syrup into cornstarch. Cook and stir over medium heat till mixture is thickened and bubbly; cook 2 minutes more.

Remove the mixture from heat; stir in butter or margarine and nutmeg. Whip cream. Top the cake with whipped cream, then the drained peaches. Pass peach sauce. Makes 6 servings.

Peach Preserve Cake

½ cup butter or margarine
1 cup sugar
½ cup peach preserves
2 eggs
2 cups sifted all-purpose flour
2 teaspoons baking powder
1 teaspoon salt
½ teaspoon ground cinnamon
¼ teaspoon baking soda
1 teaspoon grated orange peel
½ cup orange juice
  Peach Frosting

Cream first 3 ingredients thoroughly. Add eggs; beat till fluffy. Sift together dry ingredients. Add to creamed mixture alternately with the combined orange peel, juice, and ¼ cup water; beat after each addition. Bake in greased and lightly floured 13x9x2-inch pan at 350° till done, about 35 minutes. Cool. Frost the cake with Peach Frosting.

Peach Frosting: Cream ¼ cup butter with ⅓ cup peach preserves. Gradually add 2 cups sifted confectioners' sugar; beat till fluffy.

Pizza-Peach Pie

½ cup butter or margarine
¼ cup sifted confectioners' sugar
1 cup sifted all-purpose flour
2 tablespoons cornstarch
2 tablespoons granulated sugar
¼ teaspoon ground mace
⅔ cup orange juice
½ cup red currant jelly
1 29-ounce can sliced peaches, well drained

For crust, cream together butter or margarine and confectioners' sugar. Blend in flour to make soft dough. Pat evenly onto bottom and sides of 12-inch pizza pan; prick well with fork. Bake at 350° for 15 to 20 minutes.

For filling, combine cornstarch, granulated sugar, and mace in small saucepan. Stir in orange juice; add jelly. Cook and stir till mixture is thickened and bubbly; cook 2 minutes more. Cool. Arrange peaches in single layer in baked shell, forming circles, one inside the other. Spoon glaze over. Chill. Trim with whipped cream, if desired. Serves 10 to 12.

Cherry-topped fresh or canned peach halves are surrounded with an apricot-sherry glaze for tart-style Petite Peach Pies. Sweetened whipped cream is passed for a topping.

Peach Pie

Prepare Plain Pastry for 9-inch lattice-top pie (See *Pastry*). Combine ¾ to 1 cup sugar, 3 tablespoons all-purpose flour, ¼ teaspoon ground nutmeg *or* cinnamon, and dash salt. Add to 5 cups sliced fresh peaches; mix. Line 9-inch pie plate with pastry; fill. Dot with 2 tablespoons butter. (Dash with extra spice, if desired.) Adjust lattice crust; seal and crimp edges. Bake at 400° for 45 to 50 minutes. Serve the pie while it is still warm.

Petite Peach Pies

    1 *teaspoon* unflavored gelatin
    2 tablespoons cold water
    1 12-ounce jar apricot preserves
    ¼ cup cream sherry
    4 *ripe* peaches, peeled and halved,
        or 1 29-ounce can peach halves,
        well drained
    8 *baked* 3½-inch pastry shells
    8 stemmed maraschino cherries
    ½ cup whipping cream, whipped

Soften gelatin in water. Heat preserves to boiling; add gelatin. Stir to dissolve. Add sherry and dash salt. Cool till slightly thickened. Place peach half, cut side down, in tart shell. Spoon preserve mixture over. Chill. Whip cream. Top each pie with cherry and cream.

Crunchy Peach Cobbler

    6 fresh peaches, peeled and
        sliced (4 cups)
    1 cup sugar
    2 tablespoons lemon juice
        • • •
    1 14-ounce package oatmeal
        muffin mix
    ¼ teaspoon ground nutmeg
    ½ cup butter or margarine

Combine peaches, sugar, and lemon juice. Turn into an 8x8x2-inch baking dish. In mixing bowl combine muffin mix and nutmeg; cut in butter till like coarse crumbs. Spoon over peaches. Bake at 375° for 40 to 45 minutes. Cut in squares. Serve warm or cool topped with ice cream, if desired. Makes 6 to 8 servings.

Fresh Fruit Bars

Substitute blueberries for raspberries next time—

    1 roll refrigerated sugar cookie
        dough
    1 8-ounce package cream cheese,
        softened
    ⅓ cup sugar
    ½ teaspoon vanilla
        • • •
    2 cups sliced peaches
    2 cups raspberries
    ¼ cup apricot preserves
    1 tablespoon water

Cut cookie dough into slices ⅛ inch thick. Arrange slices in bottom of *ungreased* 15½x10½x 1-inch baking pan or a 14-inch pizza pan, overlapping edges of dough slightly. Press to even dough. Bake at 375° for 12 minutes; cool.

In mixer bowl combine cream cheese, sugar, and vanilla; beat till smooth. Spread on cooled cookie crust; arrange peaches and raspberries on top. Combine apricot preserves and water; spoon over fruit. Chill. Cut into 3x2-inch bars or diamonds. Makes 25 bars.

Almond-Peach Torte

Combine 2½ cups sifted all-purpose flour, ½ cup finely chopped toasted almonds, ⅓ cup sugar, and ½ teaspoon salt; cut in ¾ cup butter or margarine. Gradually add ⅓ cup cold water; gently toss the mixture with a fork to moisten. Form dough in ball; divide the dough in thirds. Roll each third on *ungreased* baking sheet to ⅛-inch thickness; trim to 8-inch circles. Bake at 375° till lightly browned, about 10 to 12 minutes; cool.

Drain and chill one 30-ounce can sliced peaches and one 8¾-ounce can crushed pineapple. Whip 2 cups whipping cream with ¼ cup sugar and ¼ teaspoon almond extract; set aside 1½ cups for frosting. Reserving 6 peach slices, chop the remaining peaches and fold them with pineapple into whipped cream. To assemble the torte, spread *half* of the fruit filling on one crust, top with the second crust, add the remaining fruit filling, and third crust. Frost with reserved whipped cream. Garnish with reserved peaches and 2 tablespoons toasted slivered almonds. Makes 8 to 10 servings.

PEACH MELBA—A dessert that is made of peaches, ice cream, and a raspberry (melba) sauce. This flavorful dessert was created by the famous French chef, Escoffier, in honor of the Australian opera star, Dame Nellie Melba. (See also *Melba.*)

PEANUT—Whether they are called groundnuts, earthnuts, ground peas, or goobers, peanuts have long been a favorite with Americans. Despite its name, the peanut is not a nut. Instead, it is a vegetable related to peas and beans.

Peanuts, apparently native to Peru, have been cultivated in South America since the time of the Inca Indians. Explorers of this area transported peanut plants back to Europe and from there peanut cultivation spread to Africa.

Peanuts were exceptionally well suited to the African soil and climate, and they soon thrived to the point that the peanut plant was worshipped by some African tribes. The peanut became such a staple food of the Africans that it was one of the things that the first slaves imported into Virginia brought with them.

In the southern part of the United States, peanuts gradually became a popular crop. Most northerners, however, weren't familiar with the peanut until the Civil War when Yankee soldiers carried a fondness for it back to the North.

Although the United States is not the world's largest peanut producer, the peanut is an important crop in the South, and people all over the United States enjoy the peanut in one form or another. At least three things deserve mention in connection with the success of peanut cultivation —the boll weevil scourge on cotton, George Washington Carver's research on peanuts, and the development of mechanical harvesters in the twentieth century.

During the nineteenth century, most southern farmers concentrated on cotton as their major crop without considering the possibility that other crops might be more profitable. In 1915, however, boll weevils destroyed most of the cotton in several of the southern states. At this time, many of the farmers began planting peanuts instead of cotton. This venture proved so profitable that at least one town, Enter-prise, Alabama, erected a monument to the boll weevil in recognition of the part this insect played in the introduction of the peanut crop to the southern states.

Another vital factor in the development of peanuts as an important southern crop was the work of George Washington Carver. This famous Negro researcher not only played an important role in convincing southerners that they should plant peanuts, but he also devoted very extensive research time to developing hundreds of uses for this crop. In his laboratory at Tuskegee University in Alabama, Carver used peanuts to make numerous food products as well as by-products such as ink, dyes, insulation, detergents, and wallboard.

Until the beginning of the twentieth century, harvesting and shelling peanuts was a slow process that had to be done by hand. However, when mechanical pickers and shellers were introduced in the early 1900s, the speed-up in processing resulted in a rapid increase in the size of the peanut crop. Today, peanut harvesting and processing, like most manufacturing, is almost completely mechanized.

Nutritional value: Peanuts are an excellent source of vegetable protein. In fact, in areas such as India and parts of West Africa where animal protein is scarce but peanuts are abundant, this legume often serves as a major source of protein.

Chopped peanuts and peanut butter make Dixie Coffee Bread doubly delightful. This bread is especially good served warm.

Although a high fat content makes peanuts quite high in calories (about 85 calories in 1 tablespoon roasted peanuts), their protein content makes peanuts more nutritionally valuable than most other snack foods. Peanuts also contain appreciable amounts of the B vitamins, niacin, riboflavin, and thiamine, and minerals.

Types of peanuts: In the United States the majority of the peanut crop is made up of three types of peanuts—Virginia, Spanish, and Runner.

Virginia peanuts have a large pod that contains two rather large, oblong seeds. Its other distinctive features are the light red skin that covers the seed and the characteristic constriction of the pod between the seeds. This type of peanut is especially prized for roasting in the shell and salting out of the shell.

Like the Virginian, the pod of Spanish peanuts contains two seeds and is constricted between the seeds. However, the seeds are smaller and rounder than those of the Virginian and are covered with a pinkish tan to light tan skin. Spanish peanuts are used mainly in candies, confections, and salted nut mixtures.

Although about the same size as Spanish peanuts, Runner peanuts are characterized by the lack of pod constriction between the two seeds. A light, reddish brown skin covers the seeds. This type of peanut is generally made into peanut butter, peanut oil, or salted nut mixtures.

How peanuts are processed: Understandably, the first step in processing peanuts is harvesting them. This operation is divided into parts—digging, drying, and picking. The digging part of harvesting involves cutting the peanut vines at the stem and then pulling the pods, still attached to the vine, from the ground. Once they have been dug up, the peanuts must be dried, either by the sun and wind or mechanically. The last part of harvesting is picking the peanuts from the vine. A combine or a stationary picker is used for this.

After the peanuts have been harvested, they are transported to huge manufacturing plants. Here they are cleaned, usually shelled, roasted, and processed further, if necessary, to produce marketable forms such as whole roasted peanuts, salted peanuts, and peanut products.

The three most important peanut products are peanut flour, peanut oil, and peanut butter (see also *Peanut Butter*). Peanut flour, made of finely ground peanuts, is sometimes used with all-purpose flour in baked goods. High-grade peanut oil is used alone as a salad or cooking oil. It is also one of the ingredients in hydrogenated vegetable shortening, cooking and salad oil blends, and margarine.

How to select and store: The form of peanuts you select depends largely on how you are going to use the peanuts. Although raw peanuts, either unshelled or shelled, are occasionally available, almost all peanuts are roasted before being marketed. Not only are roasted peanuts available in the shell, but you can also find roasted, shelled peanuts, with or without the thin, crispy, brown skins, and roasted, shelled, salted peanuts, by themselves or mixed with other nuts. Both vacuum-packed dry-roasted peanuts and roasted, de-fatted peanuts are also widely available.

When choosing peanuts still in the shell, look for clean, bright shells that are free of blemishes. Shape is not a reliable indicator of quality. As with unshelled peanuts, the appearance of shelled peanuts is the best selection guide. Look for shelled peanuts that are free of blemishes and not overly darkened from roasting.

Although vacuum-packed peanuts will keep for long periods of time on the kitchen shelf, other peanuts are much more perishable. Store them in the refrigerator and use them within a short time.

How to use: The popularity of both unshelled and shelled peanuts is so widespread in the United States that this snack is permanently associated with at least two activities—sports events and the circus. Vendors at these events sell numerous packages of peanuts, and the crowd at the circus is sometimes permitted to feed peanuts to the hungry elephants.

However, peanuts aren't limited only to use as a snack food. They are an essential ingredient in one of America's favorite hard candies, peanut brittle. Broiled fish fillets become extraordinarily tasty when topped with chopped peanuts, and chocolate fudge or cake frosting is especially delicious when you add some peanuts. Peanuts also add texture as well as a delightful flavor to dishes such as desserts, main dishes, and salads. (See *Legume, Nut* for additional information.)

Peanut-Bran Bars

A no-bake cookie—

    1 cup sugar
    ⅓ cup creamy peanut butter
    2 well-beaten eggs
    3 cups bran flakes
    ½ cup peanuts
    ¼ cup semisweet chocolate pieces
    1 tablespoon light corn syrup
    2 teaspoons water

In skillet stir together sugar, peanut butter, and eggs. Cook over medium heat, stirring constantly, till mixture comes to a boil and pulls away from sides of skillet. Stir in bran flakes and peanuts, mixing thoroughly. Turn into a buttered 9x9x2-inch pan. Spread mixture evenly in pan. Chill till firm, 2 to 3 hours.

In small saucepan combine chocolate pieces, corn syrup, and water. Cook and stir over very low heat till chocolate is melted and mixture is smooth. Drizzle melted chocolate mixture over top of chilled mixture in zigzag pattern. Cut in bars. Makes 2 dozen.

Dixie Coffee Bread

In mixing bowl sift together 1½ cups sifted all-purpose flour, ¼ cup sugar, 4 teaspoons baking powder, and ½ teaspoon salt. Stir in ¾ cup cornmeal. Add ¾ cup milk, 2 slightly beaten eggs, and ½ cup melted shortening, cooled. Stir till just blended. Pour into greased 9x9x2-inch pan. Bake at 400° for 15 minutes.

Spread Peanut Topper over baked bread; sprinkle with ½ cup coarsely chopped peanuts. Bake 5 minutes. Cut in squares. Serve warm.

Peanut Topper: Blend together ½ cup brown sugar and ½ cup peanut butter. Gradually add ⅓ cup milk, beating till fluffy.

Goober Cookies

    ⅔ cup shortening
    1 cup brown sugar
    1 egg
    1 cup sifted all-purpose flour
    ½ teaspoon salt
    ½ teaspoon baking powder
    ½ teaspoon baking soda
    1 cup quick-cooking rolled oats
    ½ cup wheat flakes
    ½ cup chopped salted peanuts

In mixing bowl thoroughly cream together shortening, brown sugar, and egg. Sift together all-purpose flour, salt, baking powder, and baking soda; combine thoroughly with creamed mixture. Stir in quick-cooking rolled oats, wheat flakes, and chopped salted peanuts.

Roll dough into small balls; flatten slightly on greased cookie sheet. Bake at 400° till done, about 8 to 10 minutes. Cool slightly; remove from baking sheet. Makes 3 dozen.

Peanut Brittle Pie

    ⅔ cup brown sugar
    1 envelope unflavored gelatin
        (1 tablespoon)
    Dash salt
    1¾ cups milk
    2 slightly beaten egg yolks
    2 tablespoons butter or margarine
    1 teaspoon vanilla
    2 egg whites
    2 tablespoons granulated sugar
    ½ cup whipping cream
    ½ cup crushed peanut brittle
    1 9-inch *baked* pastry shell,
        cooled (See *Pastry*)

In saucepan combine brown sugar, gelatin, and salt. Stir in milk and egg yolks. Cook and stir over medium heat till gelatin dissolves and mixture thickens slightly. Add butter or margarine and vanilla. Chill, stirring occasionally, till the mixture is partially set.

Beat egg whites to soft peaks; gradually add sugar, beating to stiff peaks. Whip cream. Fold partially set gelatin mixture, crushed peanut brittle, and whipped cream into beaten egg whites. Chill till mixture mounds. Pile into cooled pastry shell; chill till firm.

Easy-Peanut Chews

    1 stick piecrust mix
    ¾ cup brown sugar
    ½ teaspoon vanilla
    1 slightly beaten egg
    ½ cup chopped peanuts

Prepare piecrust mix according to package directions. Blend in brown sugar and vanilla. Add egg and ¼ *cup* chopped peanuts. Spread on well-greased and floured cookie sheet to 13x10-inch rectangle. Top with remaining peanuts. Bake at 350° till done, about 15 to 17 minutes. *Loosen edges as soon as the cookies are removed from the oven.* Cool the cookies on sheet. Cut the cookies in bars or in squares.

Banana-Brittle Dessert

Whip 1 cup whipping cream. Peel 2 fully ripe bananas; slice thinly. Fold bananas, ¾ cup crushed peanut brittle, and 1 teaspoon vanilla into the whipped cream. Spoon into sherbets. Chill about 1 hour. Makes 4 servings.

Peanut Crunch Pie

    2 tablespoons butter or margarine,
        melted
    ½ cup sugar
    3 beaten eggs
    ½ cup light corn syrup
    ½ cup dark corn syrup
    1 teaspoon vanilla
    1 *unbaked* 9-inch pastry shell
        (See *Pastry*)
    1 cup chopped salted peanuts

Combine butter or margarine, sugar, eggs, corn syrups, and vanilla; mix till well blended. Pour into *unbaked* pastry shell; sprinkle with peanuts. Bake at 375° for 10 minutes. Reduce heat to 350°; bake 35 to 40 minutes more.

Happy snacking

← Hungry teen-agers will devour these Double Peanut Butter Cookies after a tennis match or any time. They're also an adult favorite.

Peanut-Cereal Candy

    3 cups crisp rice cereal
    1 cup salted peanuts
    ½ cup sugar
    ½ cup light corn syrup
        . . .
    ½ cup peanut butter
    ½ teaspoon vanilla

Mix cereal and peanuts; set aside. In saucepan combine sugar and corn syrup. Cook, stirring constantly, till mixture comes to a full rolling boil. Remove mixture from heat.

Stir in peanut butter and vanilla. Immediately pour syrup over the cereal mixture, stirring gently to coat. Pat the cereal evenly into a buttered 8x8x2-inch pan. Cool the candy; cut it in 2x1-inch bars. Makes 32 bars.

PEANUT BUTTER—A spread made of ground, roasted peanuts. At first, peanut butter marketed in this country was unhomogenized and known for its ability to "glue the teeth together." Today, however, peanut butter, both creamy and chunk-style, is homogenized and has lost much of this objectionable sticky quality.

Since peanuts are native to South America, it is not at all surprising that South Americans were the first ones to make a type of peanut butter by grinding peanuts and mixing them with honey or cocoa. Nevertheless, the first peanut butter used in the United States was not an adaptation of the South American product. Rather, a St. Louis physician is credited with developing it as a nutritious (it is especially high in vegetable protein), easily digestible food for his patients. As soon as other people found out how delicious this new food was, it became popular as a food for everyone. In fact, today, the popularity of peanut butter is so great that millions of peanut butter sandwiches are eaten daily.

As is evidenced by its highly popular use in sandwiches, peanut butter is most commonly used as a spread. Although a simple sandwich made of peanut butter on bread is delicious, make your peanut butter sandwich even better by adding jam, jelly, soft cheese, or a meat spread. For a change, try spreading peanut butter on

Chunk-style peanut butter turns packaged cake mix and canned or homemade frosting into an unusual Peanut Butter Crunch Cake.

toast, muffins, biscuits, or celery sticks. Or use it instead of mayonnaise or butter on canapés and meat sandwiches.

This highly nutritious spread is equally good as a flavoring ingredient in many other dishes such as cookies, candies, breads, and desserts. Peanut butter added to a cream soup or a fruit salad dressing makes a delightful dish. Chocolate and peanut butter are particularly complementary in candies, puddings, dessert sauces, and cake frostings. Peanut butter muffins are also delicious. As can be seen, you can create all kinds of peanut-buttery dishes; just use a little imagination.

Peanut Butter Swirls

In saucepan combine 1 cup brown sugar, ⅓ cup milk, ¼ cup light corn syrup, and 1 tablespoon butter. Cook and stir till sugar dissolves and butter melts; remove from heat.

Add ¼ cup peanut butter. Beat till smooth; cool. In parfait glasses alternate layers of sauce and vanilla ice cream (begin and end with ice cream). Top with peanuts. Serves 4.

Double Peanut Butter Cookies

1½ cups sifted all-purpose flour
½ cup sugar
½ teaspoon baking soda
¼ teaspoon salt
½ cup shortening
½ cup creamy peanut butter
¼ cup light corn syrup
1 tablespoon milk
Peanut butter

Sift together flour, sugar, baking soda, and salt. Cut in shortening and the ½ cup peanut butter till mixture resembles coarse meal. Blend in light corn syrup and milk. Shape into 2-inch roll; chill. Slice ⅛ to ¼ inch thick. Place *half* the slices on *ungreased* cookie sheet; spread each with ½ teaspoon peanut butter. Cover with remaining slices; seal edges with fork. Bake at 350° for 12 minutes. Cool slightly; remove from sheet. Makes 2 dozen.

Peanut Butter and Jelly Cake

A traditional combination in a new form—

2 cups sifted all-purpose flour
1½ cups sugar
3 teaspoons baking powder
1 teaspoon salt
⅓ cup shortening
⅓ cup peanut butter
1 cup milk
2 eggs
1 10-ounce-jar currant jelly (about 1 cup)
1 package fluffy white frosting mix
½ cup chopped peanuts

In mixer bowl sift together flour, sugar, baking powder, and salt. Add shortening, peanut butter, and milk; beat 2 minutes at medium speed on electric mixer. Add eggs and beat mixture 2 minutes more. Pour into greased and floured 13x9x2-inch baking pan. Bake at 350° till cake tests done, 45 to 50 minutes. Cool.

Break up jelly with a fork; spread evenly over cake. Prepare frosting mix according to package directions. Carefully spread frosting over jelly on cake; sprinkle with chopped nuts. Cut the cake in squares to serve.

Peanut Butter Crinkles

A great cookie jar filler—

½ cup butter or margarine
½ cup granulated sugar
½ cup brown sugar
½ cup chunk-style peanut butter
1 egg
½ teaspoon vanilla

. . .

1¼ cups sifted all-purpose flour
¾ teaspoon baking soda
¼ teaspoon salt
Granulated sugar
Salted peanuts, halved

In mixing bowl thoroughly cream together butter, sugars, peanut butter, egg, and vanilla. Sift together flour, baking soda, and salt; blend into creamed mixture. Shape dough in 1-inch balls; roll in granulated sugar. Place 2 inches apart on greased cookie sheet. Press a few peanut halves on balls of dough. Bake cookies at 375° for 8 to 10 minutes. Cool slightly on cookie sheet; remove to rack to cool completely. Makes about 4 dozen cookies.

Refreshing Peanut Butter Swirls are quickly prepared from a simple peanut butter sauce, vanilla ice cream, and chopped peanuts.

Peanut Butter Crunch Cake

1 package 2-layer-size yellow cake mix
½ cup chunk-style peanut butter
3 eggs
1⅔ cups milk
Nutty Chocolate Frosting *or* Speedy Frosting

In mixer bowl combine yellow cake mix, chunk-style peanut butter, eggs, and milk. Blend at low speed of electric mixer; beat 2 minutes at medium speed. Turn into a greased 13x9x2-inch baking pan. Bake at 350° till done, about 35 to 40 minutes. Cool. Frost cake with Nutty Chocolate Frosting *or* Speedy Frosting.

Nutty Chocolate Frosting: Combine one 16-ounce package sifted confectioners' sugar, ½ cup unsweetened cocoa powder, and ¼ teaspoon salt. Add ⅓ cup boiling water, ⅓ cup butter or margarine, and ¼ cup peanut butter; blend. Add 1 teaspoon vanilla; blend.

Speedy Frosting: In mixing bowl blend one 16½-ounce can chocolate frosting and ¼ cup chunk-style peanut butter.

Peanut Buttered Pork

A grilled specialty—

Tie 5 to 6 pounds boned pork loins together at 1½-inch intervals with fat sides out. Balance roast on spit and secure with holding forks; insert meat thermometer. Season with salt and pepper. Arrange *medium* coals at rear of firebox; knock off ash. Place a foil drip pan in front of coals and under roast. Attach spit, turn on motor, and lower hood. Roast till thermometer registers 170°, about 3 hours.

Combine ½ cup orange juice and ¼ cup creamy peanut butter. When thermometer reads 170°, brush with sauce on roast and continue cooking 15 to 20 minutes. Serves 15.

PEANUT FLOUR—A finely ground meal made from dried, roasted peanuts. (See *Flour, Peanut* for additional information.)

PEANUT OIL—A vegetable oil extracted from chopped, cooked, shelled peanuts. (See *Oil, Peanut* for additional information.)

PEAR

*Suggestions on how to make good things to eat
with this "butter fruit."*

Once called "gift of the gods" by Homer, the well-known poet of ancient Greece, pears have been and still are among the most popular fruits of the world. Fossil remains indicate that this fruit was known thousands of years prior to the civilization of man. Today, hundreds of pear varieties are classified, although relatively few ever appear in American supermarkets. These core fruit, all oblong in shape and usually larger at the blossom end than at the stem end, are close relatives of apples.

Pears originated on two separate fronts: western Asia/eastern Europe, and eastern Asia. Each area developed a distinctive and commercially important variety. The European pear, *Pyrus communis*, is the species from which most of the sweet, juicy pears of today are descended. The sand pear, *Pyrus pyrifolia*, first grew wild in eastern Asia and is today the foundation of many popular pear hybrids.

Although seemingly not as popular a fruit as the early apple varieties, pears were used by Stone Age men. Archaeological remains from Swiss lake dwellings indicate the use of pears in this region, and remains from Asia Minor suggest that pears were grown in Hittite orchards, too.

The number of European pear varieties increased rapidly once Greek and Roman civilizations began pear cultivation. Pears were common to Greece by 300 B.C. As Rome grew in governmental strength, Roman writers recorded an increasing number of varieties being developed. Both Greeks and Romans ate fresh and dried pears as well as pear conserves.

Thanks to the conquering Romans, pears were introduced to other temperate regions of Europe and subsequently became an important food. The Frankish King, Charlemagne, ordered that pear trees be planted in home gardens and, thus, pear trees were grown extensively in castle and monastic orchards. During the 1700s and the 1800s, the French and Belgians developed many new varieties.

Pears were brought to the North American continent as the territory was colonized. Pilgrims brought pears to New England; the French, to lands near the Detroit River. Spanish missionaries introduced pears to Mexico and gradually northward to California. By 1771, a large, Long Island fruit nursery listed 42 pear varieties.

But in 1780, pear trees in the East suffered a similar fate to the grapes in California—extinction by a disease. In this case, it was a disease called fire blight. The plight of orchards in the East appeared very grave as more and more trees died.

To a great extent pear cultivation in the United States was saved by the east Asian sand pear (so named because its very hard flesh has many sand or grit cells). Although sand pear trees first grew wild in Manchuria and Mongolia, they were later cultivated in China and Japan. Sand pears were then taken to Europe, and by 1850 had been introduced to the United States. Although the fruits were (and still are) very distasteful, sand pear trees were resistant to fire blight. Chance crossings of sand and European pears were the beginnings of hybrids like Kieffer pears that produced trees that were resistant to blight, yet with excellent fruit for eating.

Plush pears

← Fresh pears are attractively featured in two taste-tempting desserts—red-tinted Baked Crimson Pears and Pear Crumble Pie.

How pears are produced: Today, commercial pear production areas in the United States are located in both eastern and western regions. Hybrid pears that are resistant to fire blight are grown extensively in the eastern states, particularly in New York and Michigan. In Oregon, Washington, and California, the main western-producing states, European pear varieties are of primary commercial importance.

The propagation and cultivation of pears is similar to that of apples. Seedling rootstocks are started from pear cores, which are available from pear canneries. The desired pear variety is then budded onto the seedling rootstocks. To enable the trees to grow and strengthen, they are allowed to develop several years before they are permitted to bear fruit. Careful pruning and training during the early growth of the trees permit a certain amount of control of tree size and shape.

Pear trees can tolerate a fairly wide range of growing conditions. They thrive on well-drained, moderately textured soil, but they are less resistant to cold weather

The basket in back holds greenish yellow Anjous and Fall Russets (like Boscs) with long, tapering necks, cinnamon brown skins, and sweet, spicy flavor. The front oval basket contains the larger red-blushed Comice pears and shapely red-tinted Bartletts.

than are apple trees. Pear trees, however, can live and continue bearing fruit for as long a period as 75 years.

Like bananas, pears are harvested before they are fully ripe. If pears are allowed to ripen on the tree, the flesh becomes very mealy or gritty, depending on the variety. The optimum picking period is when the fruits readily separate from the twigs of the tree without breaking the stems from the fruits.

After harvesting and sorting, pears are placed in refrigerated storage. Since they can maintain their quality in these chilled conditions for some time, pears are available in grocery stores for a considerable period of time each year.

Nutritional value: Pears are a storehouse of beneficial nutrients. The caloric content (1 medium pear, 3x2½ inches, contains about 100 calories) comes mainly from carbohydrates. Fructose, the sweetest of all carbohydrates, is present in pears in a greater amount than in any other fruit. The cellulose in pears aids the digestive process. The vitamins and minerals, available in a balanced assortment, include vitamin A, the B complex, vitamin C, iron, copper, calcium, and phosphorus.

Types of pears

The eighteenth- and nineteenth-century French and Belgians were instrumental in the development of pear varieties on a widespread scale. In fact, it was the style of the times to see who could produce the greatest number of new varieties. Nicholas Hardenpont, a Belgium priest, grew the first pears with a flavor that was to give pears the name "butter fruit." At about this same time, Jean Baptiste vass Mans, a Belgian physician, began hybridizing pears on a large scale. By 1866, a British botanist had listed 850 pear varieties, 683 of which were European in origin. Many of these early types have since been forgotten, but the ones most outstanding in flavor still survive in improved forms.

Pear varieties are categorized according to the time of year in which they are harvested. Summer or early-fall pears include the Bartlett and Seckel pears. Winter pears, those harvested during late fall or winter, include Anjou, Bosc, Comice, and the Winter Nelis varieties.

Many of the varieties popular today can serve dual purposes, fresh and cooked. Use recommendations are based on a general concensus of opinion and should not be considered as hard and fast rules. (For information concerning a specific variety, see the chart on page 1620.)

How to select and store

Canned and dried pears can be enjoyed any time of the year and are easily bought and stored. Fresh pears, more limited in availability (the largest share from August to November) must be carefully checked at purchase time and must be stored properly if the fruit is to taste good.

Fresh pears are selected primarily by how they look and feel. Skin color is not a good indication of ripeness since color is dependent on the pear variety. Surface spots, especially on the sides or blossom ends, are one indication that the flesh may be corky. Choose bruise- and cut-free pears that are fairly firm to the touch, yet are beginning to soften. Avoid pears that are excessively hard and those that are wilted and shriveled with dull skins and weak areas near the stem ends.

Pear storage is dependent on the ripeness of the fruit. If the pears are still underripe, let them remain at room temperature for a few days until they are of the desired ripeness. Use slightly underripe fruit for cooking, and reserve the fully ripe ones for eating uncooked. Fully ripe pears should be refrigerated until they are used and are satisfactorily stored in this manner for about one week.

How to prepare

Pears require some thoughtful preparation in order that they are as attractive as possible. In some cases, the peel must be removed; in others, the core. Cut pears must be treated to prevent the surfaces from losing the pure white color.

Whether or not to peel pears is determined by the intended use and personal preference. When eating pears as a snack fruit or when using pears in salads, select unpeeled pears. They are just as tasty and, often, much more decorative. On the other hand, cooked in sauces or baked dishes, pears are usually peeled for better aesthetic and taste appeal.

Pear Waldorf Salad

2½ cups diced unpeeled pears
1 tablespoon lemon juice
1 cup diced celery
½ cup raisins
¼ cup coarsely chopped walnuts
¾ cup mayonnaise or salad
    dressing

Sprinkle pears with lemon juice and dash salt. Add celery, raisins, and nuts. Toss with mayonnaise; chill. Makes 6 to 8 servings.

Pears used whole, halved, or sliced are sometimes cored. For whole pears, carefully remove the core with an apple corer. (For whole pears filled with a stuffing, this procedure is necessary, but whole pears without a filling are often baked, core and all. The soft, uncooked flesh separates readily from the core.) For cut pears, slice the pears in half. Remove the center cores with a melon ball cutter or a ½ teaspoon measure. When sliced pears are desired, try the all-in-one operation, using the specially designed slicer-corer.

Baked Crimson Pears

4 medium fresh pears
1 cup low-calorie cranberry juice
    cocktail
3 inches stick cinnamon
10 drops red food coloring

Peel, halve, and core pears; place in 1-quart casserole. In saucepan combine remaining ingredients. Bring to boiling; pour over pears. Bake, covered, at 350° for 20 minutes, turning pears after first 10 minutes. Uncover; turn pears. Bake till pears are tender, 5 to 10 minutes longer. Remove cinnamon stick. Serve warm or chilled in sauce. Makes 8 servings.

		Favorite Pear Varieties		
Variety	Availability	Appearance	Flavor	Uses
Anjou	October-May	Medium to large; chunky, short neck; thin, light to yellow green skin.	Rich, spicy; juicy; smooth textured.	Fresh, cooked, or canned.
Bartlett	July-October	Medium; bell-shaped; creamy yellow skin with red blush.	Fine-grained; aromatic; juicy.	Fresh or canned.
Bosc	September-March	Large; long, tapering neck; dark yellow skin overlaid with cinnamon brown to golden russet.	Buttery smooth; rich, slightly tart.	Fresh, baked, or broiled.
Comice	October-March	Medium to large; thick neck; pale green to yellow skin blushed with red.	Aromatic; sweet, juicy.	Fresh.
Seckel	September-December	Small; skin is richly russeted.	Sweet.	Fresh or canned.
Winter Nelis	February-May	Medium; light green skin with russet specks.	Very sweet.	Fresh, cooked, or canned.

Maintaining the color of fresh pears can be achieved in several ways. The cut pears can be immersed in a sugar syrup, treated with ascorbic acid color keeper as the label directs, or brushed with citrus or pineapple juice mixed with some water. One of the favorite, yet simple methods of preparing pears, poaching them in a flavored liquid or syrup or baking them with a sauce, also helps to keep fresh pears from becoming discolored.

How to use

The popular uses of pears span meals from breakfast to bedtime snack. Their mild flavor blends well with many different foods and flavorings, and thus, pear combinations can be molded to suit the taste of most all individuals.

Breakfast ideas using pears are one way to welcome the family to a cheery morning. Enhance a pear-fruit combo with cream and a few flecks of cinnamon. Use pear slices atop cereal or use pears as the basis for a taste-tempting coffee cake.

Pear Coffee Cake

    1 16-ounce can sliced pears,
        drained
    1 teaspoon lemon juice
    ½ cup sugar
    ½ cup all-purpose flour
    ¼ teaspoon ground cinnamon
    ¼ cup butter or margarine
    1 14-ounce package orange
        muffin mix

Sprinkle pears with lemon juice. Mix next 3 ingredients; cut in butter till mixture is crumbly. Prepare muffin mix, using package directions. Turn into greased 9x9x2-inch pan. Top with pears; sprinkle with flour mixture. Bake the cake at 400° for about 30 to 35 minutes.

At lunch or dinner, pears are favored for salads, accompaniments, and desserts. Vary their use from one course to another to give pleasing diversity to menus.

Favorite combinations for side dish or main dish salads include pears with cottage cheese, with cream cheese balls rolled in nuts, or with blue cheese. For a different touch, mix pears with other fruits such as melons, apples, bananas, cherries, peaches, and grapes in arranged or tossed salads. Or embed pears in shimmering fruit-flavored gelatin molds.

Sherry-Spiced Pears

   1 29-ounce can pear halves
   1 cup brown sugar
  ½ cup dry sherry
   2 tablespoons vinegar
   1 tablespoon chopped candied
      ginger
  ¼ teaspoon ground cinnamon

Drain pears, reserving ½ cup syrup. In saucepan combine reserved syrup, brown sugar, sherry, vinegar, ginger, and cinnamon. Stir mixture over medium heat till sugar is dissolved. Add the drained pear halves and simmer 5 minutes. Serve pears either hot or cold.

Pink Pear Salad

   1 29-ounce can pear halves,
      chilled
   8 drops red food coloring
   2 3-ounce packages cream
      cheese, softened
   1 tablespoon finely chopped
      candied ginger
    Stick cinnamon

Drain pears, reserving syrup; dry on paper toweling. Add food coloring to ¼ cup water; dab on pears to tint. Combine *1 package* cream cheese with ginger; beat with enough reserved syrup to make fluffy. Use cheese mixture to fill pear hollows and to seal 2 pear halves together. Using the other package of cream cheese in a cake decorator, pipe ruffles around the sealed edge of pears. Add tiny stick cinnamon stems. Makes 4 servings.

Middle East Pears

   1 29-ounce can pear halves
      chilled and drained
   1 cup plain yogurt
  ¼ cup sugar
    Ground nutmeg *or* cinnamon

Place pear halves on lettuce-lined plates. Combine yogurt and sugar; spoon into pear cavities. Sprinkle with nutmeg or cinnamon.

Pear-Pineapple Ring

   1 29-ounce can pear halves
   1 3-ounce package orange-
      pineapple-flavored gelatin
   1 cup boiling water
   2 tablespoons lemon juice
  ¼ teaspoon salt
  ¼ teaspoon ground ginger
  ¼ cup chopped walnuts
   1 3-ounce package cream cheese,
      softened
   5 canned pineapple slices, halved
    Thin strips canned pimiento

Drain pears, reserving 1 cup syrup. Dissolve gelatin in boiling water. Stir in reserved pear syrup, lemon juice, salt, and ginger. Chill till partially set. Meanwhile, stir nuts into cream cheese; shape in small balls. Place one ball in center of each pear half.

Overlap pineapple slices and pear halves in 6½-cup ring mold with cut side of pear toward center. Arrange pimiento strips between. Pour gelatin mixture over all. Chill the mixture until firm. Makes 8 to 10 servings.

Purchasing pears

The following figures will assist you in determining how many pears to buy:

  1 pound equals 3 to 4 medium pears

  1 pound equals 2 cups diced or sliced pears

  2 to 3 pounds yields about 1 quart canned or frozen pears

Pear-Blue Cheese Salad

    3 cups diced unpeeled fresh
      pears
    1 cup diced celery
    ½ cup broken walnuts
        •   •   •
    1 ounce blue cheese, crumbled
      (¼ cup)
    ¼ cup dairy sour cream
    ¼ cup mayonnaise or salad dressing

Combine pears, celery, and nuts. Blend remaining ingredients and dash salt; toss lightly with pear mixture. Makes 6 to 8 servings.

Creamy Pear-Lime Mold

Prepare half of a ⅞-ounce package (1 envelope) low-calorie lime-flavored gelatin, following package directions. Beat one 3-ounce package softened Neufchatel cheese with 2 tablespoons skim milk; slowly add gelatin, beating till light and foamy. Chill till partially set. Fold in one 16-ounce can dietetic-pack pear halves, drained and diced, and 1 medium banana, peeled and sliced. Pour into 4½-cup mold. Chill gelatin-fruit mixture till firm. Makes 6 servings.

Jewel-like cranberries intermingle with spicy sauced pears and halved orange slices for mint-garnished Rosy Pear Compote.

Pear Salad with Cheese Dressing

    1 cup mayonnaise
    ½ cup buttermilk
    1 thin slice onion
    1 teaspoon Worcestershire sauce
      Dash garlic powder
    1 cup crumbled blue cheese
    4 unpeeled fresh pears, halved
      and cored
      Leaf lettuce
    1 11-ounce can mandarin oranges,
      drained and chilled

Place mayonnaise, buttermilk, onion, Worcestershire sauce, and garlic powder in blender container; add *half* the blue cheese. Cover container; blend just till smooth. (Dressing will become thin if blended too long.) Stir in remaining cheese; chill. Arrange pear halves on lettuce. Fill centers with mandarin oranges; pass blue cheese dressing. Makes 8 servings.

Pears as accompaniments add sparkling notes to meats. Halves filled with mint jelly team well with lamb; fruit-glazed halves, with pork; and cranberry relish-filled halves, with poultry.

For dessert, pears are suave and gourmet finales even when simply prepared. Delicately flavored pears are suitable with sauces, in puddings, pies, cakes, cobblers, and dumplings. (See also *Fruit*.)

Baked Pears Elegante

    2 medium fresh Bartlett pears
    ½ cup port
    ¼ cup sugar
    1½ inches stick cinnamon
    3 whole cloves
      Dash salt
    3 thin lemon slices

Peel, halve, and core pears; place in 1-quart baking dish. In a saucepan combine remaining ingredients; add a few drops red food coloring, if desired. Bring to boiling; pour over pears. Bake, covered, at 350° for 20 minutes. Uncover; bake till tender, basting once or twice, about 10 minutes. Serve hot, or chill. Top with whipped cream, if desired. Makes 2 servings.

Rosy Pear Compote

    1 16-ounce can whole cranberry
       sauce
    ⅓ cup sugar
    1 tablespoon lemon juice
    ¼ teaspoon ground cinnamon
    ¼ teaspoon ground ginger
    6 fresh pears, peeled, cored,
       and quartered
    2 medium oranges, peeled, sliced,
       and halved

In medium saucepan combine first 5 ingredients; bring mixture to boiling. Place pears and oranges in a 1½-quart casserole or baking dish. Pour cranberry mixture over pears and oranges. Cover and bake at 350° till the pears are tender, about 40 minutes. Spoon the fruit into sherbets. Garnish with mint sprigs, if desired. Serve warm. Makes 6 servings.

Chocolaty Meringue Pears

    6 fresh pears
    ½ cup water
    ¼ cup sugar
    ¼ cup apricot jam
    2 tablespoons dry sherry
    2 teaspoons lemon juice
    2 tablespoons chopped maraschino
       cherries
    1 tablespoon dry sherry
    1 egg white
    3 tablespoons sugar
    1 1-ounce square semisweet chocolate

Peel pears; core and trim bottoms so that the pears will stand up. Combine water, ¼ cup sugar, jam, 2 tablespoons dry sherry, and lemon juice. Cook and stir till sugar dissolves, about 5 minutes. Add pears to apricot mixture; cover and simmer till tender, about 20 minutes, stirring occasionally. Meanwhile, soak cherries in the 1 tablespoon dry sherry.

Remove pears to shallow baking dish, reserving ½ cup cooking liquid. Fill pear centers with cherries. Beat egg white till soft peaks form; gradually add 3 tablespoons sugar, beating to stiff peaks. Swirl meringue atop each pear. Bake at 350° till browned, 12 minutes. Add chocolate to reserved liquid; heat and stir till melted. Spoon over pears. Serves 6.

Cream-Topped Pears

Blend ½ cup dairy sour cream and 1 to 2 tablespoons grenadine syrup. Spoon over 8 chilled canned pear halves. Makes 4 servings.

Ginger-Pear Crumble

    3 fresh pears, peeled, halved,
       and cored, *or* one 16-ounce
       can pear halves, drained
       Lemon juice
    ¾ cup fine gingersnap crumbs
    ¼ cup brown sugar
    2 tablespoons butter or margarine,
       melted
       Dash salt
       Vanilla ice cream
       Maraschino cherries

Place pear halves, cut side up, in 8-inch pie plate. Sprinkle fresh pears with 1 teaspoon lemon juice *or* canned pears with 1 tablespoon lemon juice. Combine crumbs, brown sugar, butter, and salt. Sprinkle over top of pears. Bake at 350° till pears are tender and hot, about 25 minutes. Serve warm or cold. Top each serving with ice cream and a cherry. Serves 6.

Chocolaty Meringue Pears are doubly sauced. They're cooked in an apricot-sherry blend, then served with chocolate sauce.

Midwinter Fruit Medley

　　1　16-ounce can peach halves,
　　　　drained
　　1　16-ounce can pear halves,
　　　　drained
　　6　lettuce cups
　　1　8¾-ounce can pineapple
　　　　tidbits, drained
　　　　Seedless green grapes
　　1　11-ounce can mandarin oranges,
　　　　drained
　　2　bananas, sliced
　　　　Pitted dates, halved
　　　　Honey Dressing

Arrange individual servings of peach and pear
halves in lettuce cups. Fill centers and sur-
round with remaining fruits. Pass Honey Dressing. Makes 6 servings.

　　Honey Dressing: In small mixer bowl mix ¼
cup sugar; 1 teaspoon each dry mustard, paprika, and celery seed; and ¼ teaspoon salt.
Add ⅓ cup vinegar, ⅓ cup honey, 1 tablespoon
lemon juice, and ½ teaspoon grated onion.
Pour 1 cup salad oil into mixture very slowly,
beating constantly with rotary or electric mixer.

Rosy Pear Sundaes

　　1　10-ounce jar currant jelly
　　1　tablespoon cornstarch
　　1　teaspoon grated orange peel
　⅓　cup orange juice
　　4　to 6 drops red food coloring
　　　　　　． ． ．
　　1　pound fresh pears, peeled
　　　　and sliced (2 cups)
　　1　quart vanilla ice cream

Melt jelly in saucepan. Combine cornstarch,
peel, juice, and food coloring. Stir this mixture
into melted jelly. Cook and stir till thickened
and bubbly. Add sliced pears; chill several
hours. Serve over ice cream. Serves 6 to 8.

Blue cheese and pear merger

The cavities of fresh pear halves are piled
full of mandarin oranges and placed on romaine for Pear Salad with Cheese Dressing.

Surprise Pear Bundles

4 fresh pears
1 package refrigerated crescent
   rolls (8 rolls)
4 teaspoons red cinnamon candies
2 tablespoons sugar

Peel and core pears, leaving whole; set aside. Separate refrigerated dough into 4 rectangles, sealing diagonal perforations. Place 1 pear upright on each rectangle. Fill center of each pear with *1 teaspoon* cinnamon candies; sprinkle *1½ teaspoons* sugar over each.

Moisten edges of dough; bring up around whole pears and seal tightly. Grease four 6-ounce custard cups *or* four 2¾-inch muffin cups thoroughly. Place one pear dumpling in each, seam side up. Bake at 425° for 10 minutes; reduce oven temperature to 350° and bake dumplings 20 minutes more. Place each dumpling in serving dish; serve warm with light cream or ice cream, if desired. Makes 4 servings.

Pears Helene Cake

Fancy dessert made fast using convenience foods—

½ cup butter or margarine
½ cup brown sugar
1 16-ounce can pear halves
16 pecan halves
16 maraschino cherries
1 package 2-layer-size yellow
   cake mix
1 can ready-to-spread chocolate
   frosting

Grease and flour one 9x1½-inch round pan. In a second 9x1½-inch round pan melt butter. Remove from heat; sprinkle brown sugar over butter. Use *4 pear halves* and ¼ *cup syrup from pears;* slice pears lengthwise into thirds. Arrange with nuts and cherries in butter mixture.

Add water to reserved ¼ cup pear syrup to equal liquid called for on package of cake mix. Using syrup mixture, prepare cake mix according to package directions; divide batter between pans. Bake according to package directions. Invert pan with pears on wire rack; cool both layers about 10 minutes before removing pans. With frosting, frost plain layer; cover with fruited layer. Frost sides of both layers.

Pear Crumble Pie

6 medium Bartlett pears, peeled
3 tablespoons lemon juice
½ cup sugar
2 tablespoons all-purpose flour
1 teaspoon grated lemon peel
1 9-inch *unbaked* pastry shell
   (See *Pastry*)
   • • •
   Crumble Topping
3 slices sharp process American
   cheese

Slice 5 pears; cut remaining pear in sixths. Sprinkle pears with lemon juice. Mix sugar, flour, and peel; stir into sliced pears. Spoon into pastry shell. Arrange pear wedges atop sliced pears. Sprinkle with Crumble Topping. Bake at 400° till pears are tender, 45 minutes. Remove from oven. Cut cheese slices in half diagonally and arrange on pie. Serve warm.

Crumble Topping: In mixing bowl mix ½ cup all-purpose flour, ½ cup sugar, ½ teaspoon *each* ground ginger and cinnamon, and ¼ teaspoon ground mace. Cut in ¼ cup butter or margarine till the topping is crumbly.

Pear-Pineapple-Cheese Pie

1 16-ounce can sliced pears
1 20½-ounce can pineapple tidbits
¼ cup sugar
3 tablespoons quick-cooking tapioca
4 ounces sharp process American
   cheese, shredded (1 cup)
¼ teaspoon vanilla
   Dash ground ginger
1 *unbaked* 9-inch pastry shell
   (See *Pastry*)
½ cup dairy sour cream
1 tablespoon confectioners' sugar

Drain sliced pears, reserving ½ cup syrup; cut pears into 1-inch pieces. Drain pineapple, reserving ½ cup syrup. Combine reserved syrups, sugar, and quick-cooking tapioca in saucepan. Cook and stir over medium heat till mixture thickens and bubbles. Remove from heat and stir in cheese, vanilla, and ginger. Add pears and pineapple; turn into pastry shell. Bake at 400° for 35 to 40 minutes. Cool. Combine sour cream and sugar; spoon dollops atop pie.

PEARL BARLEY—A market form of barley in which each cereal grain has been husked and polished. Pearl barley requires long, slow cooking and is used primarily in soups. (See also *Barley*.)

PEARL TAPIOCA—A market form of tapioca in which the starch from the cassava plant is shaped into round pellets. Pearl tapioca is used as a thickening agent in preparing puddings and desserts. (See also *Tapioca*.)

PEARS HELENE—A French dessert in which pears are poached in a vanilla syrup. After cooling, the pears are served with vanilla ice cream and a warm chocolate sauce.

PECAN—The edible nut produced by a tree having the same name. Classified as a hickory, the pecan tree is a member of the walnut family. The shell of the nut has a mottled appearance that varies in hardness and thickness, while the nutmeat has an oily texture and a fine flavor.

Historians believe that the American Indian was the first to use this fruit as part of his diet. Indian names for the nut included *neces* and *nogules*. Spanish explorers in the mid 1500s noted that this new kind of soft-shell nut was very popular with the Indians living along the river banks throughout the southern part of the United States. They described the nut as being about the size of a thumb and unlike any other edible nut they had known in their homeland.

Early French explorers didn't mention pecans, and it was not until the early 1700s that Jean Penicant, a ship's carpenter, labeled the flavorful nut, *pacane*. Later French explorers described the nuts as being very delicate in flavor and less rich in oil than nuts which were common in France. References were made also to the excellent use of the nuts in pralines, a French delicacy popular in New Orleans.

Until the eighteenth century, pecans were noted only in writings of explorers who travelled in the southern regions of the United States. In 1712, Jesuit missionaries who had established a mission in southern Illinois, recorded in their writings an abundance of pecans in the immediate area surrounding their settlement.

French and Spanish explorers, although fascinated by the rather mysterious nut, did not send seeds back to Europe. This came much later. John Bartram, a botanist from Philadelphia, is credited with sending the first pecans from America to Europe. Upon his return from a trip to Ohio in 1761, he forwarded a package of seeds, commonly known as Illinois hickory or nut, to a friend in London. At about the same time, fur traders from Ohio introduced the nut to eastern settlers.

The first known planting of pecans was made in 1772 by William Prince on Long Island. A short time later plantings were made by George Washington at Mount Vernon. Previous to this time, all of the pecans in the East were secured from the plantings found along the Illinois and Ohio rivers. However, in 1799 Thomas Jefferson received seedlings from Louisiana, which he planted at Monticello.

Although many plantings were made in subsequent years, it is not known when commercial planting of pecans began. It is known, however, that in 1847 a slave gardener in Louisiana successfully grafted pecan trees, which eventually resulted in over 100 varieties. This accomplishment made possible the pecan industry.

How pecans are produced: For hundreds of years, the pecan tree has grown wild along river banks, creeks, and dry bed streams. Its natural habitat in the United States extends along the Mississippi River from southwest Texas up to the Illinois and Ohio rivers into southern Indiana. The tree is also indigenous to the Mexican highlands. The wild trees are generally unattended and, in some cases, are impossible to reach due to other wild vegetation that surrounds them. The seedling pecan, the name given to the uncultivated variety, is usually smaller in size and more shabby looking than those that are cultivated. Likewise, the shell of the nut is thicker on the seedling pecan, which results in a smaller nutmeat yield.

Since the first grafting of the pecan in 1847, cultivated orchards of different pecan varieties have developed throughout the southeastern portion of the United States. Growing areas extend from Georgia as far west as New Mexico, with the greatest production in Texas and Oklahoma.

The cultivated trees are popular not only for their nut production, but also for their appearance. It is not uncommon to find pecan trees carefully tended in large southern cities of the United States. Under optimum temperature and soil conditions, the trees may grow to a height of 160 feet with a trunk diameter of 6 feet, thus offering an attractive and cooling shade in warm climates of the United States.

The wood of the pecan tree is used along with other hickory varieties in furniture, flooring, veneers, and paneling. Pecan wood is often selected in preference to black walnut, which is much more expensive, yet similar in appearance. Most of the pecan wood comes from the wild trees from the southern Mississippi Valley.

The fruit of the cultivated pecan excels the wild nut both in appearance and in size, making it a favorite for home use, for fancy nut counters, and for commercial gourmet needs. The wild pecan is sold mainly to commercial bakeries, ice cream manufacturers, and other food processors where nut appearance is not important.

Most varieties of pecan trees have their greatest production every two years. The harvest generally begins in late October and continues into late winter. The most modern method of removing the nuts from the trees is with a "shaker," a specialized

Pecan-Raisin Pie, a favorite on any table, features a surprise layer of raisins under the pecan topping. To shortcut preparation time, prepare crust from a packaged pastry mix.

machine that shakes the tree, causing the nuts to fall. Other methods employed to some degree are collecting the nuts that have fallen to the ground naturally, and using a long bamboo cane to knock the pecans from the trees.

The harvested pecans are then transported to the nut processors where they are cracked, shelled, graded, dried, and packaged. If left unshelled, the pecans are graded, cleaned, polished, and inspected before marketing. The market for in-shell pecans is greatest during the winter holiday season. However, about 85 percent of the nuts are shelled before they are packaged and readied for market.

Nutritional value: Pecans contain calcium, phosphorus, iron, protein, carbohydrate, and some vitamins. Since they are usually eaten in small quantities, however, their nutritive value serves primarily as a supplement to a well-balanced diet. Relatively high in calories, one-fourth cup of shelled pecan halves contains 174 calories.

How to store: Shelled pecans are best stored in the refrigerator in a covered container. If vacuum-packed, they require no refrigeration until after opening. Since nuts are relatively high in fat, they may become rancid if stored at warm temperatures or unrefrigerated for long periods of time. Store unshelled pecans at room temperature in a cool, dry place. If held for a long period of time, refrigerate the pecans in order to maintain freshness.

If shelled pecans are purchased in quantity, they are easily frozen for later use. To freeze, place in a tightly covered freezer container or plastic bag. Thaw at room temperature, allowing any moisture that collects to evaporate.

How to use: Pecans are a favorite ingredient in many dishes and an excellent choice in recipes that do not call for a specific type of nut. Pecans add crunch to salads, stuffings, casseroles, vegetable dishes, and desserts. A popular ingredient in fudge and other confections, pecans add flavor and interest to home-baked yeast breads, sweet rolls, quick breads, cookies, cakes, and appetizers.

Toasted pecans are excellent sprinkled over hot soups or salted lightly and served alone as a snack. For an attractive garnish, arrange pecan halves or sprinkle chopped pecans over pies, cakes, cookies, puddings, and sundaes. (See also *Nut.*)

Southern Pecan Pie

    3 eggs
    ⅔ cup sugar
       Dash salt
    1 cup dark corn syrup
    ⅓ cup butter or margarine, melted
    1 cup pecan halves
    1 *unbaked* 9-inch pastry shell
       (See *Pastry*)

Beat together first 5 ingredients; stir in nuts. Pour into pastry shell. Bake at 350° till knife inserted halfway between center and edge comes out clean, about 50 minutes. Cool.

Pecan-Raisin Pie

    1 cup light corn syrup
    3 tablespoons sugar
    1 tablespoon butter or margarine
    ⅛ teaspoon salt
    1 cup evaporated milk *or* light cream
    3 beaten eggs
    1 cup chopped pecans
    1 teaspoon vanilla
    ½ cup raisins
    1 *unbaked* 9-inch pastry shell
       (See *Pastry*)

Combine first 4 ingredients. Cook and stir till boiling; cook and stir 1 minute more. Remove from heat; stir in milk. Cool. Slowly stir into eggs; blend well. Stir in nuts and vanilla. Sprinkle raisins on bottom of pastry shell; top with filling. Bake at 400° for 35 minutes.

Fresh from the oven

Caramel-Pecan Rolls, generously topped→ with pecan halves, are a welcome treat served at breakfast or for a morning break.

No need to wait for the holidays to serve homemade candy. Caramel-flavored Pecan Log offers an unbeatable flavor at any time.

Pecan Tassies

    1 3-ounce package cream cheese,
         softened
    ½ cup butter or margarine,
         softened
    1 cup sifted all-purpose flour
              • • •
    ⅔ cup coarsely broken pecans
    1 egg
    ¾ cup brown sugar
    1 tablespoon butter or margarine,
         softened
    1 teaspoon vanilla
         Dash salt

In mixing bowl blend together cream cheese and ½ cup butter; stir in flour. Chill 1 hour. Shape into twenty-four 1-inch balls; place in *ungreased* 1¾-inch muffin pans. Press dough against the bottom and sides of the pan. Sprinkle *half* of the pecans over dough.

Beat together egg, brown sugar, 1 tablespoon butter, vanilla, and salt till smooth. Spoon egg mixture atop "tarts." Top with remaining pecans. Bake at 325° till filling is set, 25 minutes. Cool; remove from pans. Makes 24.

Pecan Crispies

    ½ cup butter or margarine,
         softened
    6 tablespoons brown sugar
    6 tablespoons granulated sugar
    1 egg
    ½ teaspoon vanilla
    1¼ cups sifted all-purpose flour
    1 teaspoon baking powder
    ¼ teaspoon baking soda
    ¼ teaspoon salt
    1 cup chopped pecans

In mixing bowl cream together butter, brown sugar, and granulated sugar till light and fluffy. Beat in egg and vanilla. Sift together flour, baking powder, baking soda, and salt; blend into creamed mixture. Stir in pecans. Drop from teaspoon on *ungreased* cookie sheet. Bake at 375° for 10 minutes. Cool slightly before removing from pan. Makes 30.

Apple-Raisin Cake

    ½ cup butter or margarine
    2 cups sugar
    2 eggs
              • • •
    2½ cups sifted all-purpose flour
    1½ teaspoon baking soda
    1 teaspoon salt
    1 teaspoon ground cinnamon
    ½ teaspoon ground nutmeg
    ¼ teaspoon ground allspice
    1½ cups canned applesauce
    ½ cup raisins
    ½ cup chopped pecans
         Orange-Butter Frosting

Cream butter and sugar till fluffy. Add eggs one at a time, beating well after each. Sift together flour, and next 5 ingredients. Add alternately to creamed mixture with applesauce. Stir in raisins and pecans. Turn into greased and lightly floured 13x9x2-inch baking pan. Bake at 350° about 45 minutes. Cool in pan.

Frost with *Orange-Butter Frosting:* Cream 6 tablespoons butter or margarine, softened with 1 teaspoon grated orange peel and dash salt. Beat in 3 cups sifted confectioners' sugar and enough orange juice (about 3 tablespoons) to make of spreading consistency.

Pecan Log

    1 12-ounce package butterscotch
        fudge mix
    8 ounces caramels (about 28)
    ¼ cup milk
    1½ cups chopped pecans

Prepare fudge mix according to package directions; cool. Roll cooled fudge into four rolls about 1 inch in diameter. In saucepan heat and stir caramels with milk over low heat till caramels melt. Spread fudge rolls with caramel mixture; roll in chopped pecans. Chill. Cut rolls in ½-inch slices. Makes 32 slices.

Quick Pecan Rolls

    1 cup brown sugar
    2 tablespoons dark corn syrup
    ½ cup butter or margarine, melted
    ⅔ cup broken pecans
        . . .
    3 cups sifted all-purpose flour
    ⅓ cup granulated sugar
    4½ teaspoons baking powder
    1 teaspoon salt
    ½ cup shortening
    2 slightly beaten eggs
    ⅔ cup milk
        . . .
    2 tablespoons butter or margarine,
        melted
    ¼ cup granulated sugar
    1 teaspoon ground cinnamon

Combine brown sugar, corn syrup, and ½ cup melted butter or margarine; divide mixture among 18 muffin cups. Sprinkle with pecans.

Sift together flour, ⅓ cup granulated sugar, baking powder, and salt. Cut shortening into dry ingredients. Add slightly beaten eggs and milk all at once; stir just to blend.

Turn dough out on lightly floured surface; knead 8 to 10 times. Roll into 15x12x¼-inch rectangle. Brush with 2 tablespoons melted butter or margarine; sprinkle with mixture of ¼ cup granulated sugar and cinnamon. Roll up jelly-roll fashion, beginning with long side; seal edges. Cut into ¾-inch slices. Place slice, cut side down, in each muffin cup. Bake at 375° for 20 to 25 minutes. Remove rolls from pans immediately. Makes 18.

Caramel–Pecan Rolls

    2 packages active dry yeast
    5½ to 6½ cups sifted all-purpose
        flour
    2¼ cups milk
    3 tablespoons shortening
    2 tablespoons granulated sugar
    1 tablespoon salt
        . . .
    1 cup brown sugar
    ½ cup butter or margarine, melted
    2 tablespoons corn syrup
    1 cup pecan halves
        . . .
    ¼ cup butter or margarine,
        softened
    ½ cup granulated sugar
    1 teaspoon ground cinnamon

In large mixer bowl combine yeast and *2½ cups* of the flour. In saucepan heat milk, shortening, 2 tablespoons granulated sugar, and salt just till warm, stirring occasionally to melt shortening. Add to dry mixture in mixing bowl. Beat at low speed with electric mixer for ½ minute, scraping sides of bowl constantly. Beat 3 minutes at high speed.

By hand, stir in enough of the remaining flour to make a soft dough. Turn out onto lightly floured surface; shape into a ball. Knead till smooth and elastic, about 5 to 10 minutes. Cover with clear plastic wrap, then a towel; let rest 20 minutes. Punch down.

Meanwhile, in small saucepan combine brown sugar, melted butter, and corn syrup; cook and stir till blended. Distribute mixture in bottom of 36 well-greased muffin pans (or three 9-inch round cake pans); top with pecans.

Divide dough in half; roll each portion to a 16x10-inch rectangle. Spread each rectangle with *half* the softened butter or margarine. Mix ½ cup granulated sugar and cinnamon; sprinkle sugar-cinnamon mixture over dough.

Roll up jelly-roll fashion, beginning with long side; seal edges. Cut into 18 slices. Place rolls, cut side down, in prepared pans. Cover with oiled waxed paper, then clear plastic wrap; refrigerate 2 to 24 hours.

When ready to bake, remove rolls from refrigerator; let stand 20 minutes. Just before baking, puncture any surface bubbles with greased wooden pick. Bake at 425° for 20 to 25 minutes. Invert on cooling racks. Makes 36.

PECTIN—A carbohydrate that is present in fruit. An important ingredient in the making of jelly and jam, pectin produces a gel when it is combined with sugar and fruit juice in the correct proportions.

The pectin content of fruit varies with the ripeness of the fruit. As the fruit ripens, the amount of pectin increases. But when the fruit reaches maturity, chemical changes cause a decrease in the amount of pectin. Therefore, when the maximum amount of pectin is needed, as for jelly, use fruit that is slightly underripe.

Pectin content also varies with the variety or type of fruit. For example, fruits considered high in pectin include crab apples, sweet and sour apples, cranberries, currants, grapes, gooseberries, grapefruit, lemons, limes, loganberries, sour blackberries, sweet and sour guavas, sour plums, sour oranges, and quinces. Fruits low in pectin are apricots, bananas, elderberries, pineapple, rhubarb, pears, sour peaches, and strawberries.

Since the pectin content of fruit is not always known, the addition of commercial pectin is recommended for making most jellies and jams. Prepared primarily from apples and citrus fruits, commercial pectin is available in powdered and liquid forms. Excellent results are obtained by using either form. Because the method for using each type varies, it is important to follow package directions closely. Liquid pectin must be used within a few days after opening. Powdered pectin, which has a longer storage life, remains stable for several months after opening.

Generally, a larger yield is obtained when commercial pectin is used in making jellies and jams. This increased yield is the result of a shorter cooking time, which reduces the amount of juice loss through evaporation. Furthermore, the preparation time is shorter and a more consistent product is obtained. (See also *Jelly*.)

PEEL—1. The outer skin, rind, or covering on fruits and vegetables. 2. To remove the outer skin or rind from a food.

PEMMICAN—A concentrated food made from a mixture of dried meat, dried fruit, and fat. First prepared by the American Indian to carry on hunting trips, pemmican originally consisted of buffalo meat or venison, wild berries, and tallow or animal fat. The mixture was shaped into cakes.

Today, pemmican is used as an emergency ration and is prepared from dried beef, dried fruit (prunes, apricots, raisins, and currants), herbs, and refined fats other than butter. When properly prepared and sealed, pemmican keeps almost indefinitely and provides excellent nourishment in a compact food product.

PENNSYLVANIA DUTCH COOKERY—The regional cuisine that has developed over the last 300 years in the predominantly Germanic settlement in southeastern Pennsylvania. Characterized as "good food of good people," Pennsylvania Dutch cookery offers a thrifty, yet appealing approach to the preparation and serving of food.

Many of the Pennsylvania Dutch dishes are a combination of imagination and artistry, such as shoofly pie. Prepared from molasses, brown sugar, flour, and spices, the rich flavor of this pie has escaped duplication outside of the Pennsylvania Dutch kitchen. Another contribution of this ingenious and thrifty cuisine is flavorful potato-custard pie.

Traditionally, dinner in the Pennsylvania Dutch home is accompanied by "seven sweets and seven sours." Friends and neighbors are often invited to join family members at the table to relish the good food of the land. Frequently included among the "sweets and sours" are spiced peaches, pickled beets, sweet potato relish, sauerkraut, homemade pickles, apple butter, fox-grape jelly, honey cake, and a variety of decorated cakes and cookies.

An abundance of good food

A Pennsylvania Dutch meal offers a variety → of sweets and sours. Shown here, from top to bottom, are Lebkuchen (see *Lebkuchen* for recipe), spiced peaches, pickled beets, Apple Butter (see Apple for recipe), coleslaw, Veal and Carrots, Shoofly Pie (see *Shoofly Pie* for recipe), Berks County Potato-Custard Pie, and Sweet Potato Relish.

Substantial and hearty, the dishes of the Pennsylvania Dutch are prepared from foods found in abundance in the rural setting. Scrapple, Philadelphia pepper pot, chicken-corn soup, sauerkraut, *schnitz-un-knepp,* waffles, and buckwheat cakes are only a few of the more familiar favorites closely linked to the early settlers in southeastern Pennsylvania. Although there is little time for the more frivolous and glamorous dishes, a meal occasionally includes caviar along with an assortment of homemade specialties, such as parsnip fritters.

The Pennsylvania Dutch people, to whom food is very important, are Germanic in origin. The result of a mixture of Swiss, Moravians, and Hollanders, these people came together in America to seek a new way of life and opportunity.

The first Pennsylvania Dutch settlement, planned by William Penn, was composed of Mennonites. Known as Plain People, the Mennonites founded Germantown near Philadelphia in 1683. Their early experience in farming proved beneficial to them in the New World. They selected land dotted with black walnut trees, the presence of which indicated that the ground had a limestone-rich soil—a sign of good farmland. Shortly after this, other Plain People from the Palatinate (a province of the Rhineland in Germany) arrived from Europe and settled in the fertile farmland of southeastern Pennsylvania. These people included the Amish, Dunkers or Brethren, Moravians, Schwenkfelders.

Although the early settlers were industrious and thrifty, in the beginning they were forced to live off fish, game, and the fruits that grew wild in the area. A shortage of food was not uncommon during the early years, and milk, butter, and flour were considered luxuries. Out of necessity, their cooking was even plainer and simpler than that to which they were accustomed in their old homelands. In time, however, they enjoyed bountiful harvests and adapted the cooking techniques of their forefathers to their new environment.

By the eighteenth century, other Dutch people, known as the "fancy" Dutch, began to arrive from the Old World. Together, the "fancy" Dutch and the Plain People built what today is known as the Pennsylvania Dutch culture. The two factors that kept the Pennsylvania Dutch united and that separated them from the other settlements in the New World were the German dialect that they shared, and their common reverence for food coupled with respect for the productive farming land.

A very inventive people, the Pennsylvania Dutch were particularly adept at perfecting equipment and tools useful in securing or producing food. They designed a new rifle for shooting game; built the Conestoga wagon for transporting surplus food to neighboring markets; cast the first American cookstove; and developed a long-handled waffle iron for use over a fire.

The popularity of the Germanic settlers' cooking spread throughout the colonies. Presidents George Washington and James Buchanan found favorites among the Pennsylvania Dutch specialties. Furthermore, the baking of these people was esteemed so highly that the honor of baker general of the Continental Army was awarded to a Pennsylvania Dutch baker.

Except for the advent of the railroad, which replaced the wagon for transporting surplus food to market, the nineteenth century brought little change to the lives of the Pennsylvania Dutch. Although a few of the people moved to cities, most were content to remain within their own communities, tilling the land and enjoying their freedom. An almost totally self-sufficient people, their dependence on the country store was limited to coffee, sugar, salt, pepper, and other spices.

During the spring months of each year, large gardens were planted to meet the family's needs, in addition to allowing a surplus for marketing. When ripe, many of the vegetables such as beets, turnips, potatoes, and pumpkins were stored for use in the winter. Large orchards provided a wide variety of fruit. Some of the fruits, including raspberries and blackberries, were dried on large, hot, brick hearths. The dried fruit was a favorite made into pies during the fall and winter months.

Apples were the basis for many regional dishes, including apple soup, apple cider, and apple butter. Fried apples, another delicacy, were made from choice apples and sprinkled with cinnamon and confectioners' sugar before eating. Dried apple slices, known as schnitz, were popularly used as chewing gum before the introduction of the commercial product. Another favorite use of apples was schnitz-un-knepp, a substantial and hearty main dish prepared with dried apple slices, dumplings, and ham or pork.

A traditional fall activity was the making of sauerkraut. Usually served with pork, it was originally prepared by stomping the cabbage with bare feet, although today kraut-making is much more refined.

The cold winter months were ideal for butchering hogs. Special woods were selected for smoking different parts of the animal, as each wood imparted a characteristic flavor to the meat. Being very thrifty, the Pennsylvania Dutch made use of each part of the pig: the feet were jellied; the meat scraps were made into scrapple, the lard was used for frying; the hog bristles were sold; and the choice meat cuts were presented to helpful neighbors and friends at Christmas.

Many foods were gathered from the surrounding countryside, including walnuts, which were either pickled or used in baking. Likewise, chestnuts were a popular ingredient in stuffings prepared for fowl. Dandelions were the basis for making wine, while the greens were prepared in a special salad served during Holy Week.

Making butter and cheese were continuous activities throughout the year in every household. The butter was shaped in a mold that carried the family insignia. Kitchen shelves were lined with a variety of homemade preserves and condiments, such as ginger pears and pickled oysters.

As noted previously, baking was an important task in the Pennsylvania Dutch kitchen. Every homemaker had an assortment of recipes for sweet breads, dumplings, noodles, cakes, cookies, and pies. Each credited her success in baking to an ingredient, such as a kind of sugar.

The holidays, celebrated with large feasts, were particularly joyous occasions for the Pennsylvania Dutch. Traditional Christmas foods included a variety of cookies, doughnuts, sand tarts, candies, and *Lebkuchen*—a dessert prepared with honey, almonds, citron, and orange peel.

Special doughnuts called fastnachts were served on Shrove Tuesday. Sometimes made with a hole in the center, fastnachts were fried in lard, which was saved for healing open wounds.

Eggs were eaten in quantity at Easter and were featured at egg-eating contests. The Pennsylvania Dutch were the first to link the brightly colored egg-tree, of Germanic origin, to Easter celebrations. Bright colors and fancy designs were transferred to the eggs by first wrapping the eggs in flowered calico, then boiling.

Another Pennsylvania Dutch specialty was cornmeal mush. Using a special method for preparing the mush, they preferred to use yellow meal that had been roasted before grinding. After many hours of long, slow cooking, the mush was served either warm with cold milk, or cold with warm milk. If fried, the mush was topped with pure maple syrup, comb honey, or spicy apple butter. A traditional Pennsylvania Dutch breakfast for guests included fried mush, fried apples, and sausage.

The Shakers, who were also Plain People, lived a short distance from the Pennsylvania Dutch, but they were not considered a part of the settlement since they were of English origin. "Shaker dried corn," prepared and sold to the Pennsylvania Dutch by the Shakers, is often found among Pennsylvania Dutch recipes, even though it originated outside of the settlement. The corn was prepared by baking it for several days either in the sun or in the oven. Then it was soaked for several hours, salted, simmered, and eaten with cream and butter. Even today, Shaker dried corn is used by the Pennsylvania Dutch in preference to fresh corn when preparing many of their favorite corn dishes.

The Pennsylvania Dutch cuisine is carried on today by many of the descendants of the Amish sect. In keeping with their strict religious beliefs, many of the descendants maintain their farms as food factories without the conveniences of electricity and telephones. Guests share in the rich Pennsylvania Dutch heritage and enjoy good food produced in abundance. The cuisine offers an adventure in good eating, unlike that found elsewhere throughout the country. Fortunately, many of the traditional dishes of the Pennsylvania Dutch have transcended the original boundaries of the settlement. Thus, many of the foods readily identified with this cuisine are enjoyed in other areas, too.

Sweet Potato Relish

   3 cups chopped, peeled, cooked
       sweet potatoes
   2 cups fresh whole kernel corn *or*
       one 16-ounce can whole kernel
       corn, drained
   1 16-ounce can limas, drained, *or*
       one 10-ounce package frozen
       baby limas, cooked and drained
   2 cups chopped green pepper
   2 cups chopped onion
2½ cups brown sugar
1½ cups vinegar
   1 tablespoon salt
   2 teaspoons celery seed
   1 teaspoon ground turmeric
   ⅛ teaspoon pepper

In 10-quart kettle combine all ingredients. Bring to boiling; reduce heat to medium. Boil gently, uncovered, for 20 minutes. Seal relish in scalded jars. Makes 8 cups.

Berks County Potato-Custard Pie

   1 *unbaked* 8-inch pastry shell
       (See *Pastry*)
   2 tablespoons butter or margarine
   1 cup warm mashed potatoes
   ¾ cup sugar
   2 slightly beaten egg yolks
   ½ cup milk
   1 teaspoon grated lemon peel
   ¼ cup lemon juice
   2 egg whites

Bake unpricked pastry shell at 400° for 7 to 8 minutes. In saucepan add butter to potatoes; stir in sugar. Cool. Stir in egg yolks, milk, peel, and lemon juice; mix well. Beat egg whites till soft peaks form. Carefully fold egg whites into potato mixture. Turn into partially baked pastry shell. Bake at 375° till knife inserted halfway between center and edge comes out clean, about 35 to 40 minutes.

Veal and Carrots

1½ pounds veal round steak, ¾
       inch thick
   2 tablespoons all-purpose flour
   1 teaspoon salt
   ⅛ teaspoon pepper
   2 tablespoons shortening
   ¾ cup tomato juice
   1 cup diced, peeled carrots
   ½ cup finely chopped onion
       Hot buttered noodles

Cut veal into ¾-inch cubes. Combine flour, salt, and pepper; coat meat evenly with flour mixture. In large skillet brown meat on all sides in hot shortening. Add tomato juice, carrots, and onion. Cover and simmer till meat and vegetables are tender, about 1 hour. Serve over hot buttered noodles. Makes 5 or 6 servings.

PENUCHE (*puh nōō′ chē*), **PANOCHA** (*puh-nō′ chuh*)—A crystalline candy made with brown sugar. Golden brown in color, penuche has a smooth, creamy texture, similar to that of chocolate fudge. To make penuche, the brown sugar mixture is cooked to a soft-ball stage, cooled, and then beaten until smooth. Chopped nuts are sometimes added. (See also *Candy*.)

Penuche

1½ cups granulated sugar
   1 cup brown sugar
   ⅓ cup light cream
   ⅓ cup milk
   2 tablespoons butter or margarine
   1 teaspoon vanilla
   ½ cup broken walnuts or pecans

Butter sides of heavy 2-quart saucepan. In it combine first 5 ingredients. Cook over medium heat, stirring constantly, till sugars dissolve and mixture comes to boiling. Cook to soft-ball stage (238°), stirring only if necessary. Immediately remove from heat and cool to luke-warm (110°). *Do not* stir. Add vanilla. Beat vigorously till candy becomes very thick and starts to lose its gloss. Quickly stir in nuts; spread in buttered shallow pan. Score while warm; cut when firm.

PEPPER *(spice)* — The pungent spice that comes from the berries produced by the perennial evergreen vine, *Piper nigrum*. A native to India, pepper is noted in writings that are over 3,000 years old. The cultivation of pepper began in Indonesia around 100 B. C. Since that time, production has spread throughout the tropics.

Often recognized as the most important spice in the world, pepper was a major commodity in Europe during the Middle Ages. Pepper was not only used as a seasoning, but also as a preservative, a medicine, and a medium of exchange.

The pepper vine grows to an average height of 30 feet with a stem diameter of about ½ inch. Support for the vines is furnished by young trees or by timber posts. Although berry production is limited for the first few years, the vine normally produces berries for 15 to 20 years. As the berries mature, they change color.

To make black pepper, the berries are removed when green. The berries are dried, causing the skin to shrivel and change to a deep brown or black, while the core remains light in color. Ground black pepper is a mixture of the black skin and the light core. Named after the area in which they are produced, the major types of black pepper are Malabar, Tellicherry, Lampong, Sarawak, Brazilian, and Ceylon. Each differs in flavor and pungency.

White pepper is produced from mature berries, which are soaked to loosen the skin. After the skin is removed, the white cores are dried and then ground. Milder in flavor and finer in grind than black pepper, white pepper is available in three types— Muntok, Brazilian, and Sarawak.

In order to avoid flavor loss pepper is best stored in a cool, dry place. As with other spices, the finer the grind, the shorter the storage life. If unground, pepper keeps almost indefinitely.

Sometimes used two or three times in the preparation of a single dish, pepper enhances the flavor of most foods. White pepper is preferred in dishes that are light in color, such as salad dressings, cream soups, and sauces. Although the use of white pepper has increased in recent years, it is not as widely used in the United States as it is in Europe. (See also *Spice*.)

Roast-Peppered Rib Eye

```
1  5- to 6-pound boneless rib eye
     beef roast
½ cup coarsely cracked pepper
½ teaspoon ground cardamom
1  tablespoon tomato paste
1  teaspoon paprika
½ teaspoon garlic powder
1  cup soy sauce
¾ cup vinegar
   Gravy
```

Trim excess fat from meat. Mix pepper and cardamom; rub over meat, pressing in with heel of palm. Place meat in shallow baking dish. Combine tomato paste, paprika, and garlic powder; gradually stir in soy, then vinegar. Carefully pour over meat. Cover; marinate in refrigerator overnight, basting several times.

Remove meat from marinade; reserve marinade. Let meat stand at room temperature for 1 hour. Wrap meat in foil; place in shallow roasting pan. Roast at 300° for 2 hours for medium-rare. Open foil; ladle out drippings and reserve. Brown roast, uncovered, at 350°.

Meanwhile, prepare *Gravy:* Strain reserved drippings; skim off fat. To 1 cup drippings, add 1 cup water; bring to boiling. Stir in a little reserved marinade, if desired. Serve roast *au jus.* Or mix 2½ tablespoons cornstarch with ¼ cup cold water. Stir into juice mixture. Cook and stir till thick and bubbly. Serve with meat. Makes 8 to 10 servings.

Two-Way Salad Dressing

```
3 tablespoons sugar
1 teaspoon salt
1 teaspoon dry mustard
¼ teaspoon white pepper
½ teaspoon onion juice
¾ cup salad oil
¼ cup white vinegar
```

For clear dressing: Combine all ingredients in screw-top jar. Cover and shake. Chill. Shake again just before serving. Makes 1 cup.
For creamy dressing: In small mixer bowl combine first 4 ingredients; add onion juice. At medium speed on electric mixer, beat in oil, a little at a time, alternately with vinegar and ending with vinegar. Makes 1 cup.

PEPPER *(vegetable)* — Any *Capsicum*-family plant and its fruit. The fruits of pepper plants are identified by relatively thick pods that contain numerous seeds. The diversity of shapes (elongated to round), sizes (petite to large), colors (yellow, green, red, to almost black), and flavors (sweet and mild to fiery hot) illustrates the complex make-up of this vegetable group. Bell, pimiento, paprika, and chili peppers are only a few of the varieties.

It should be realized that *Capsicum* peppers are in no way related to the black or white spice called pepper. Columbus and his fellow explorers coined the misnomer "pepper." They recognized that the pungent flavor of chili peppers, which they found growing in the West Indies, was similar to zippy peppercorns.

Many years before Columbus discovered America, hot pepper varieties were cultivated in Central and South America. Elaborate Peruvian cloths embroidered with pepper designs have been found, which indicates that peppers were used in South America over 2,000 years ago. Following Columbus' explorations, pepper use and cultivation spread first to the European continent, then to Africa and Asia, and eventually throughout the world.

From smoothing mildness to flaming hotness, peppers offer a wide span of flavor zest. Plump peppers in the back are sweet bell peppers. In the foreground are long, slender hot peppers.

How peppers are produced: Like their relative, the tomato, peppers require warm weather and much sunlight for optimum growth. The hot varieties need a long growing cycle and, thus, have not adapted well to cool regions. When milder varieties are grown in northern climates, annual plantings are required.

Peppers are picked at various stages of ripening, depending on the variety. Sweet peppers are usually harvested while they are green. Some hot peppers are yellow when picked; others are bright red.

Nutritional value: Hot peppers usually are not eaten in great enough quantities to affect nutrition. Eaten in larger amounts, sweet peppers have the advantage of being low-calorie and vitamin-packed, too. One large green pepper, uncooked, provides 22 calories, a fair amount of vitamin A, and an excellent level of vitamin C. One canned pimiento pepper has 11 calories.

Sweet peppers: Given this name because of the sweet, mild flavor, sweet peppers frequent American-style cooking more than do hot peppers. The well-known varieties of sweet peppers include bell, pimiento, paprika, and banana peppers.

Bell peppers (in the Midwest they are sometimes called mango peppers) are the kind most available to American homemakers. They may be rounded or slightly oblong with lengths and diameters varying from three to five inches. Often simply called green peppers because they are marketed while still bright green, these peppers will turn a bright red without flavor impairment if allowed to mature fully.

Confusion often arises over the use of the term pimiento peppers. In Spain, for example, pimiento peppers are considered to be a class of mild peppers. In America, on the other hand, pimiento peppers are referred to as a specific variety of pepper, mild-flavored, cone-shaped, and bright red. These natives of Europe are usually marketed either in cans or in jars.

Paprika peppers, once mostly grown in Hungary but now produced in many countries, vary in flavor strength from mild to slightly pungent, depending on the species and on the growing region. The long, thick-fleshed, bright red pods are dried and ground for use as the colorful seasoning and garnish called paprika.

Banana peppers, also called sweet green chili peppers or Italian sweet peppers, are popular with Italian cooks. These elongated peppers, tapering at the ends, range in color from green to yellow. They are often pickled and used as a relish.

How to select—Bell peppers are sold fresh, but pimiento, banana, and paprika peppers are less frequently marketed this way and are usually processed in cans or jars. A fresh pepper should have a good shape, a thick flesh, and a bright skin.

In general, the peak growing season for the sweet pepper family is from May through August, but bell peppers are now available to consumers year-round.

How to store—Fresh peppers cannot be stored for long periods of time. They must be tightly wrapped or covered and refrigerated, preferably in the vegetable crisper. Storage under colder conditions can cause peppers to lose their crispness.

How to prepare—Wash peppers in cold water before using them. Smaller varieties may be left intact if they are to be used for pickles or relishes. For larger varieties, remove the stems, seeds (these are pungent), and inner membrane. The peppers may be left whole, chopped, or sliced lengthwise or crosswise, as needed.

Occasionally, peppers to be used for baking are precooked by parboiling. This is achieved by immersing them for three to five minutes in boiling, salted water. Drain them well, then use as directed.

How to use—Sweet peppers, either uncooked or cooked, lend their pleasing flavor to many dishes. There are limitless uses for sweet peppers as appetizers—as relishes and in dips and canapés. When used whole, raw peppers can serve as the shell for dips, spreads, and salad mixtures or, when cooked, as built-in servers for meat and vegetable stuffings. Sweet peppers are popular flavorings and garnishes in salads, meat entrées, casseroles, and mixed vegetable dishes, too.

Hot peppers: Often labeled chilies or chili peppers are internationally famous for the varied potencies of pungent flavor that they provide. A particular variety's degree of "hotness" is determined by the amount of the irritating chemical, capsaicin, present. Some are so hot that they can literally burn a diner's mouth and lips. The varieties that have influenced American cooking the most are cayenne, Tabasco, and jalapeño peppers.

Species of cayenne peppers, named after but not grown in Cayenne, French Guiana, are generally characterized as being slender and from three to eight inches long, although other appearance and flavor traits vary. Red ones are dried and ground for cayenne pepper spice.

Tabasco peppers are bright red, smooth-skinned, and only about 1½ inches long. Their use in zesty sauces is well-known.

Jalapeño peppers are frequently used in Mexican cookery. They are identified by a green, smooth skin and are about two inches long. Most Americans consider jalapeño peppers to be quite hot.

How to select—Fresh hot peppers should be selected in the same manner as are the sweet varieties. The dried forms will, of course, be shriveled. Skin gloss is not affected by drying, but the coloring may be darkened considerably.

How to store—Refrigerate fresh hot peppers as you would sweet peppers. Dried hot peppers lose flavor very quickly if stored improperly. For best results, store them, tightly covered, in the refrigerator.

How to prepare—Fresh or dried hot peppers must be handled carefully. On contact with eyes or skin, the volatile oil in the peppers can create an undesirable burning sensation. With both fresh and dried hot peppers, it is recommended that rubber gloves be worn while the peppers are being handled. Avoid touching your skin or eyes during pepper preparation.

Another technique that results in a pleasant working environment is to hold the peppers under cold running water during preparation. Rinse them clean, pull out the stems, then cut the peppers in half. Remove the seeds (these are very hot) and, if desired, any extraneous membrane.

Fresh peppers may be used without further preparation, although soaking them in cold, salted water for about an hour reduces some of the intense flavor. Dried peppers must be cut in small pieces and rehydrated in boiling water for 30 minutes prior to use as a recipe ingredient. After handling hot peppers, wash your hands thoroughly with soap and water.

How to use—The precaution in the use of hot peppers is to be discreet. The amount you use depends on your tolerance to pepper pungency. Believe it or not, some people (as those who use hot peppers profusely) become immune to the intense astringency of the capsaicin.

Use of hot peppers is a notable cooking trait in many countries and regions of the world—Mexico, Latin and South America, the West Indies, India, Korea, and Indonesia to name a few. Hot peppers are frequently added to a sauce accompaniment or are used in a sauce that is cooked with the dish. In the United States, hot peppers are most often served in foreign dishes or as a relish, either plain or pickled. (See also *Vegetable*.)

Pepper Cup Trio

   3 **large green peppers**
   Spaghetti Dip
   Bacon-Blue Dip
   Deviled Dip

Cut tops from peppers; remove seeds and membranes from shells. Discard stems. Finely chop tops to equal 2 tablespoons; set aside. Fill each pepper cup with one dip. Serve with corn chips and, if desired, vegetable kabob dippers made of green pepper cubes, whole mushrooms, paper-thin cucumber slices, and cherry tomatoes.

Spaghetti Dip: Combine 1 cup dairy sour cream, the reserved chopped pepper, and 4 teaspoons dry spaghetti sauce mix. Chill.

Bacon-Blue Dip: Combine 4 ounces blue cheese, crumbled; one 3-ounce package softened cream cheese; 1 tablespoon dry white wine; and 1 teaspoon instant minced onion. Stir in ¼ cup dairy sour cream; chill. Before serving, stir in 4 strips bacon, crisp-cooked and crumbled.

Deviled Dip: With electric mixer blend together one 5-ounce jar pimiento-cheese spread, one 4½-ounce can deviled ham, ¼ cup mayonnaise or salad dressing, 1 tablespoon dried parsley flakes, 1 teaspoon instant minced onion, and 4 drops bottled hot pepper sauce. Chill.

Quick, yet imaginative dippers for Pepper Cup Trio are made by alternately spearing green pepper cubes, whole mushrooms, sliced cucumber, and cherry tomatoes on appetizer skewers.

Stuffed Pepper Cups

Cut off the tops of 6 medium-sized green peppers; remove the seeds and the membranes. Precook green pepper cups in boiling, salted water for about 5 minutes; drain them. (For crisp peppers, omit precooking.) Sprinkle the insides of the pepper cups generously with salt.

Cook 1 pound ground beef and ⅓ cup chopped onion till meat is lightly browned. Season the mixture with ½ teaspoon salt and dash pepper. Add one 1-pound can tomatoes, ½ cup water, ½ cup uncooked long-grain rice, and 1 teaspoon Worcestershire sauce. Cover and simmer the mixture till the rice is tender, about 15 minutes. Stir in 4 ounces sharp process American cheese, shredded (1 cup). Stuff the peppers; stand them upright in a 10x6x1½-inch baking dish. Bake, uncovered, at 350° for about 20 to 25 minutes. Makes 6 servings.

Chilies Rellenos Bake

In skillet brown 1 pound ground beef and ½ cup chopped onion; drain off fat. Sprinkle meat with ½ teaspoon salt and ¼ teaspoon pepper. Place one 4-ounce can green chilies, cut in half crosswise and seeded, in 10x6x1½-inch baking dish. Sprinkle with 1½ cups shredded sharp natural Cheddar cheese; top with meat.

Arrange one 4-ounce can green chilies, cut in half crosswise and seeded, over meat. Combine 4 beaten eggs, 1½ cups milk, ¼ cup all-purpose flour, ½ teaspoon salt, several dashes bottled hot pepper sauce, and dash pepper; beat the mixture till it is smooth. Pour this mixture over the chili mixture.

Bake this dish in a 350° oven till a knife inserted just off-center comes out clean, about 45 to 50 minutes. Let cool for about 5 minutes; cut in squares. Makes 6 servings.

Chicken Aloha

    1 cup chopped celery
    1 green pepper, cut in
        thin strips (¾ cup)
    2 tablespoons shortening
            •   •   •
    1 10½-ounce can condensed cream
        of chicken soup
    ½ 22-ounce can pineapple pie
        filling (1 cup)*
    ¼ cup water
    2 tablespoons soy sauce
    2 cups cubed cooked chicken
        Hot cooked rice
    ¼ cup slivered almonds, toasted

In saucepan cook celery and green pepper in hot shortening till crisp-tender. Stir in soup, pie filling, water, and soy sauce. Add chicken. Cook, stirring occasionally, till hot. Serve over hot cooked rice. Sprinkle almonds over each serving. Makes 6 servings.

*Use the remaining pie filling as a topper for cake or ice cream desserts.

Tangy Lamb Shoulder Chops

    4 lamb shoulder chops, cut
        ¾ inch thick
    1 tablespoon shortening
    ½ teaspoon salt
        Dash pepper
    ¼ cup hot-style catsup
    1 teaspoon dried basil leaves,
        crushed
    4 ½-inch thick onion slices
    4 ½-inch thick green pepper
        rings
            •   •   •
    1 ounce sharp process cheese,
        shredded (¼ cup)

Slash edges of fat on chops. In skillet brown chops on both sides in hot shortening. Sprinkle with salt and pepper. Place chops in *ungreased* 9x9x2-inch baking dish. Spread chops with catsup; sprinkle with basil. Top with onion slices and green pepper rings. Cover baking dish with foil; bake at 350° till done, about 50 minutes. Uncover; sprinkle cheese inside green pepper rings. Bake till cheese begins to melt, about 1 to 2 minutes longer. Makes 4 servings.

PEPPERCORN—The whole dried berry from the black pepper vine. Both black peppercorns and white peppercorns are available on the market. Peppercorns are frequently used whole in marinades and pickling mixtures. Ground in a home pepper mill, they lend a fresh flavor to tossed salads, vegetables, and meats. (See also *Pepper*.)

PEPPERGRASS—A type of cress that produces edible leaves used in salads or as a garnish. Peppergrass, sometimes called garden cress, is a member of the mustard family. A relative of watercress, its flavor is somewhat bitter and hot.

PEPPER MILL—A utensil used in the home to grind peppercorns. Operated by hand, a pepper mill generally produces a coarser grind than commercially ground pepper. Many pepper mills are attractively designed for use at the table.

PEPPERMINT—1. An herb used as a flavoring. 2. A confection flavored with the herb.

Although various mint flavorings have been used for centuries, peppermint was not recognized as a separate species of the mint family until the latter part of the seventeenth century. At that time, it was used primarily as a medicine. By 1840, peppermint plants were spread throughout Ohio and Michigan. Today, the cultivation of peppermint is common in many of the northern areas of the United States.

The peppermint plant reaches an average height of two to three feet and produces a pale violet flower. The leaves are bright green and have a somewhat sharper and more biting flavor than do those of the spearmint plant. The leaves are dried and marketed whole, rubbed, or in flakes.

A large percentage of the peppermint crop is used in the distillation of peppermint oil. The oil, which is relatively expensive, is light yellow and produces a

Peppermint delight

Cool and delicate Fudge Ribbon Pie features→ a chocolate-mint layer beneath a meringue studded with crushed peppermint candy.

cool sensation in the mouth due to the presence of menthol. It is commercially important in the production of candies, chewing gums, mouthwashes, toothpastes, soaps, perfumes, liqueurs, and medicines. A less-expensive oil, known as Japanese peppermint oil, is sometimes combined with the true peppermint oil. Although Japanese peppermint oil is high in menthol, it is not very flavorful.

Peppermint flavoring is an important ingredient in the preparation of many foods. The leaves are popularly used in soups, sauces, meat dishes, and vegetables. The oil, which is much more concentrated, is frequently added to candies, jellies, beverages, and desserts. (See also *Mint*.)

Fudge Ribbon Pie

      2 tablespoons butter or margarine
      2 1-ounce squares unsweetened chocolate
      1 cup sugar
      1 6-ounce can evaporated milk
      1 teaspoon vanilla
            . . .
      2 pints peppermint ice cream, softened
      1 *baked* 9-inch pastry shell, cooled (See *Pastry*)
         Peppermint Meringue

In saucepan combine butter or margarine, unsweetened chocolate, sugar, and evaporated milk. Cook and stir till chocolate melts and sauce is thick. Stir in vanilla. Cool.

Spread *1 pint* of the ice cream in pastry shell. Cover with *half* of the cooled sauce; freeze. Repeat layers with remaining ice cream and sauce. Freeze overnight or till firm.

Before serving, top with *Peppermint Meringue:* Beat together 3 egg whites, ½ teaspoon vanilla, and ¼ teaspoon cream of tartar till soft peaks form. Gradually add 6 tablespoons sugar, beating till stiff and glossy peaks form. Fold in 3 tablespoons crushed peppermint stick candy.

Remove pie from freezer. Spread meringue over chocolate layer; seal to edge. Sprinkle top with additional 1 tablespoon crushed peppermint stick candy. Place pie on cutting board. Bake at 475° till golden, about 5 to 6 minutes. Cut into wedges; serve immediately.

Peppermint Chiffon Pie

      ½ cup crushed peppermint stick candy
      ¼ cup sugar
      1 envelope unflavored gelatin (1 tablespoon)
   1¼ cups milk
      3 slightly beaten egg yolks
      ¼ teaspoon salt
      4 or 5 drops red food coloring
            . . .
      3 egg whites
      ¼ cup sugar
      ½ cup whipping cream
      1 *baked* 9-inch pastry shell, cooled (See *Pastry*)

In saucepan combine first 6 ingredients. Cook and stir over low heat till gelatin dissolves and candy melts. Tint with red food coloring. Chill till the mixture is partially set.

Beat egg whites till soft peaks form; gradually add ¼ cup sugar, beating till stiff peaks form. Fold gelatin mixture into egg whites. Whip cream; fold into egg white mixture. Chill till mixture mounds slightly. Pile into pastry shell. Chill till firm. Garnish with additional whipped cream, if desired.

Peppermint Kisses

      2 egg whites
      ½ teaspoon peppermint extract
      ⅛ teaspoon cream of tartar
         Dash salt
      ¾ cup sugar
      1 6-ounce package semisweet chocolate pieces (1 cup)

Beat egg whites, peppermint extract, cream of tartar, and salt till soft peaks form. Add sugar gradually, beating to stiff peaks. Fold in chocolate pieces. Cover cookie sheet with plain brown paper. Drop cookie mixture from teaspoon onto paper. Bake at 325° for 20 to 25 minutes. Remove from paper while slightly warm. Makes 2½ to 3 dozen cookies.

PEPPERNUT—The Americanized name for the German spice cookie better known as Pfeffernuss. (See also *Pfeffernuss*.)

How to shape peppernuts

On a board lightly dusted with confectioners' sugar, roll very stiff Peppernut dough into thin, uniform rolls about ¼ inch thick.

Place rolls of dough on a board and cut into small pieces, about ⅜ inch long. Bake cookies on cookie sheet until lightly browned.

Holiday Peppernuts are traditionally served during the holidays. Their distinctive flavor is a blend of spices and black pepper.

Holiday Peppernuts

In saucepan combine ¾ cup sugar, ⅔ cup dark corn syrup, ¼ cup milk, and ¼ cup lard; bring to boiling. Remove from heat; cool. Stir in 1 teaspoon anise extract, ½ teaspoon baking powder, ½ teaspoon vanilla, ¼ teaspoon salt, ¼ teaspoon ground cloves, and ¼ teaspoon ground cardamom. Using about 5 cups all-purpose flour, mix in enough flour to make a *very stiff* dough, kneading in the last addition. Chill.

On a board lightly dusted with confectioners' sugar, shape dough in ¼-inch thick rolls. Cut each roll in pieces ⅜ inch long; place on cookie sheet. Bake at 375° till brown, about 8 to 10 minutes. Cool 1 to 2 minutes before removing from cookie sheet. Makes 6 cups.

PEPPERONI, PEPERONI—A spicy, dry sausage of Italian origin prepared from coarsely chopped beef and pork. The seasoned meat is cured, stuffed into pork casings, and then air-dried for 3 to 4 weeks. It is marketed in twin links that measure about 1½ inches in diameter and 10 to 12 inches long. It is a favorite in pizzas, casseroles, and main dishes. (See also *Sausage*.)

Italian Spaghetti Toss

Cook 4 ounces pepperoni, thinly sliced; ½ cup chopped onion; and 1 clove garlic, minced, in 3 tablespoons salad oil till onion is tender but not brown. Cook one 10-ounce package frozen chopped broccoli following package directions; drain. Add to pepperoni mixture. Cook 6 ounces fine spaghetti following package directions; drain. Toss pepperoni mixture with spaghetti; serve with Parmesan cheese. Makes 4 servings.

Pepperoni is a favorite with pizza lovers.

PEPPER POT—1. An American stew often prepared with tripe, meat, vegetables, peppercorns, and dumplings. First served during the American Revolution, it is known also as Philadelphia pepper pot. **2.** A West Indian stew of meat and/or fish, okra, chili peppers, vegetables, and seasonings.

Pepper Pot Soup

In covered saucepan simmer ½ pound honeycomb tripe for 3 hours in water to which 1 teaspoon salt has been added for each quart of water. Drain; dice finely, making about 1 cup.

Cook ½ cup chopped green pepper, ½ cup chopped onion, and ¼ cup chopped celery in 2 tablespoons butter till onion is tender but not brown. Blend in 2 tablespoons all-purpose flour. Add 3 cups chicken broth all at once. Cook and stir till thickened and bubbly. Stir in tripe, 1 teaspoon celery salt, and ⅛ teaspoon pepper. Cover and simmer for 1 hour.

To serve, stir in ½ cup light cream and 2 tablespoons butter. Heat through. Serves 4.

PEPPER STEAK—A meat dish prepared with beef, green pepper, and tomato strips and cooked in a seasoned sauce.

Savory Pepper Steak

Cut 1½ pounds beef round steak in ½ inch thick strips. Coat with a mixture of ¼ cup all-purpose flour, ½ teaspoon salt, and ⅛ teaspoon pepper. In a large skillet brown the strips of meat in ¼ cup hot shortening.

Drain one 8-ounce can tomatoes, reserving liquid. Add reserved liquid; 1¾ cups water; ½ cup chopped onion; 1 small clove garlic, minced; and 1 tablespoon beef-flavored gravy base to meat. Cover; simmer till meat is tender, 1¼ hours. Uncover; stir in 1½ teaspoons Worcestershire sauce. Cut 2 large green peppers in strips; add to meat. Cover; simmer meat and green peppers for 5 minutes.

If sauce is too thin, combine 1 to 2 tablespoons all-purpose flour with an equal amount of cold water; stir into sauce. Cook and stir till thickened and bubbly. Add drained tomatoes, cut up; cook 5 minutes more. Serve over hot cooked rice. Makes 6 servings.

Savory Pepper Steak is a winner on any table. This saucy combo of meat and vegetables is a natural served over hot cooked rice. Long, slow simmering in a seasoned broth helps to tenderize and to flavor the meat.

PERCH—A lean fish of both freshwater and saltwater varieties that has spiny fins.

The freshwater perch family consists of about 100 species, including the walleye, white perch, and yellow perch. Both the walleye and yellow perch are known as pikeperch because of their similarity in appearance to the pike. The yellow perch is the species most commonly mentioned when talking about freshwater perch. Other names for the yellow perch are red perch, striped perch, zebra perch, and ring or banded perch. The skin of the freshwater perch is greenish gold with vertical stripes. It averages 8 to 14 inches in length and 1 to 4 pounds in weight.

The yellow perch is usually found in lakes, with most of them being caught in the Great Lakes area. They are also caught in rivers, but they prefer quiet water. The yellow perch is a popular fish with the sport fisherman.

Saltwater perch (ocean perch) are divided into two groups—Atlantic ocean perch and Pacific ocean perch. The Atlantic perch is also known as redfish or rosefish, while the Pacific perch is often called rockfish or longjaw rockfish.

The Atlantic perch prefers cold water and is found in deep water from southern Labrador to the Gulf of Maine. Its color generally ranges from orange to bright red, but occasionally it is gray or reddish brown. The ocean perch averages from 12 to 15 inches in length and most often weighs between 1 to 2 pounds.

The Pacific perch group consists of many varieties, each varying in color. Found from the Bering Sea to the lower part of California, it averages 1 to 1¾ pounds and measures 12 to 16 inches long.

Nutritional value: Freshwater perch is a lean fish and a source of protein. One medium uncooked yellow perch contains 91 calories. In the diet, it supplies some potassium, phosphorus, and the B vitamins —thiamine, riboflavin, and niacin. Ocean perch is also a lean fish and has only 95 calories for a 3½-ounce uncooked portion.

How to select: One market form for perch is the whole fish. Choose perch that has bright, clear eyes; firm flesh; and a fresh odor. The yellow perch is also available in fillets. Look for pieces that are fresh and firm, without a dried appearance.

Since most ocean perch is cut into fillets and frozen, choose fish that is tightly wrapped and solidly frozen. The fish should have little if any odor.

How to store: As is the case with other fish, fresh perch is quite perishable. Keep it iced or refrigerated and use it within two days. Solidly frozen perch will maintain quality for up to six months.

How to prepare: Perch is delicious either panfried or deep-fat fried. Likewise, it is excellent poached, steamed, broiled, or baked. If broiled or baked, remember to baste with melted butter or shortening during cooking to prevent drying. The flesh of the ocean perch is flaky and white with a delicate flavor. The flesh of the yellow perch is firm and sweet. (See also *Fish.*)

Grilled Perch with Parsley Sauce

Outdoor barbecue flavor is an added bonus—

>   2 pounds fresh or frozen perch
>   fillets
>   2 tablespoons salad oil
>   1 teaspoon salt
>   Dash pepper
>   • • •
>   ¼ cup snipped parsley
>   ¼ cup lemon juice
>   ¼ cup butter or margarine,
>   softened
>   2 tablespoons prepared mustard
>   ½ teaspoon salt

Thaw frozen fillets; cut into 6 portions. Combine salad oil, 1 teaspoon salt, and pepper; brush oil mixture over fish. Place fish fillets in well-greased wire broiler basket. Grill over *medium-hot* coals until fillets are well browned, about 4 minutes on each side.

Combine parsley, lemon juice, softened butter or margarine, prepared mustard, and ½ teaspoon salt. Spread *half* of the parsley mixture over fish. Return to grill till fish sizzles and flakes easily when tested with a fork. Serve with remaining parsley sauce. Serves 6.

Saucy Cheese-Coated Perch

    1 pound fresh or frozen perch
        fillets
 ¼ cup all-purpose flour
    1 beaten egg
    1 teaspoon salt
        Dash pepper
 ¼ cup fine dry bread crumbs
 ¼ cup grated Parmesan cheese
 ¼ cup shortening
            •   •   •
    1 8-ounce can tomato sauce
 ¼ cup water
 ½ teaspoon sugar
 ½ teaspoon dried basil leaves,
        crushed

Thaw frozen fillets. Cut into 4 portions. Coat fish with flour. Dip into a mixture of egg, salt, and pepper; then dip into a mixture of bread crumbs and cheese. In skillet fry fish slowly in hot shortening till browned on one side, 4 to 5 minutes. Turn and brown other side till fish flakes easily when tested with a fork, about 4 to 5 minutes longer.

Meanwhile, in a saucepan combine tomato sauce, water, sugar, and basil. Simmer for about 10 minutes. Serve with fish. Makes 4 servings.

A tomato-basil sauce lends a pizza flavor to Saucy Cheese-Coated Perch. The surprise in the crispy coating is Parmesan cheese.

Orange-Rice Stuffed Perch

    4 fresh or frozen pan-dressed perch
        (about ¾ pound each)
 ½ cup chopped celery
    2 tablespoons butter or margarine
 ½ cup uncooked long-grain rice
 ½ teaspoon grated orange peel
 ½ cup orange juice
    1 teaspoon lemon juice
 ½ teaspoon salt
    1 tablespoon snipped parsley
            •   •   •
    2 tablespoons butter, melted
    2 tablespoons orange juice

Thaw frozen fish. In saucepan cook celery in 2 tablespoons butter till the celery is tender. Stir in rice, ¾ cup water, orange peel, ½ cup orange juice, lemon juice, and ½ teaspoon salt. Bring to boiling; cover and reduce heat. Cook the mixture till rice is tender, 15 to 20 minutes. Stir in snipped parsley.

Sprinkle fish cavities with additional salt. Stuff *each* fish with about ½ cup orange-rice mixture. Close fish cavities by inserting skewers or wooden picks. (If necessary to hold closed, lace with string.) Combine 2 tablespoons melted butter with 2 tablespoons orange juice; brush over surfaces of fish. Place fish in well-greased shallow baking pan. Bake, uncovered, at 350° till fish flakes easily when tested with a fork, about 30 to 35 minutes. Brush fish with butter and orange juice mixture during baking. Makes 4 servings.

PERCOLATOR—A coffee maker designed to brew coffee by forcing water up a hollow stem into a basket containing ground coffee. The water, heated to boiling as it circulates, brews the coffee. Percolators may or may not be automatic. The electric percolator contains a thermostatically controlled heating unit which automatically reduces the heat to a keep-warm setting at the end of the perking cycle.

PERFECTION SALAD—A molded vegetable salad made with shredded cabbage, chopped green pepper, pimiento, and flavored with vinegar and/or lemon juice. This colorful, tart salad is a prize-winning recipe that dates back to 1904.

Pretty calico colors, biting flavor, and crunchy texture are prime examples of how ripe olive- and carrot curl-garnished Perfection Salad lives up to its flattering name.

Perfection Salad

Mix together 2 envelopes unflavored gelatin (2 tablespoons), ½ cup sugar, and 1 teaspoon salt. Add 1½ cups boiling water and stir till all ingredients are dissolved. Stir in 1½ cups cold water, ⅓ cup white vinegar, and 2 tablespoons lemon juice; chill till partially set.

Fold in 2 cups finely shredded cabbage; 1 cup chopped celery; ½ cup chopped green pepper; ⅓ cup pimiento-stuffed green olives, sliced; and ¼ cup chopped canned pimiento. Pour into 5½-cup mold. Chill till firm. Serve on lettuce-lined platter and trim with carrot curls, ripe olives, and parsley. Makes 8 to 10 servings.

PERIWINKLE—A saltwater or freshwater snail. Periwinkles are covered with a one-part shell like abalones and conches. They are found in Europe and on the eastern coast of America. (See also *Shellfish.*)

PERNOD *(pâr nō')*—A yellowish green, anise-flavored liqueur. Pernod is used as a substitute for absinthe, a liqueur of similar appearance and flavor. However, unlike absinthe, pernod is free of wormwood, a sometimes toxic oil that has banned the use of absinthe in many places. Pernod is named after the first family who manufactured absinthe. (See also *Liqueur.*)

PERRIER WATER *(per' e uhr)* — A French mineral water that is naturally well aerated and mildly alkaline.

PERRY — A still or sparkling alcoholic beverage made by fermenting pear juice. Perry, similar to hard apple cider, ranges from two to eight percent in alcoholic content and is a popular drink in Europe.

PERSIAN MELON — A muskmelon identified by fine, beige netting on a greenish gray to brown rind and by thick, orange, mildly sweet flesh. Except for its larger size and its webbed rind, the Persian melon closely resembles the cantaloupe in appearance. Although this melon's name implies that it originated in Persia, the origin of Persian melons is unknown.

Persian melons, available mainly from June to November, are selected like cantaloupe—by appearance of the rind, by the stem end, and by the aroma. When a Persian melon is ripe, the background color of the rind is free of the greenish cast, the stem end is free of any stem and has a slightly depressed scar, and there is a distinct, pleasant aroma.

If purchased mature but unripe, allow the melons to mellow at room temperature. Then, refrigerate the melons. Use ripe Persian melons within a few days.

Mild and sweet Persian melons look like oversized cantaloupes. They usually range from four to eight pounds in weight.

The characteristic flavor of Persian melons makes them an enjoyable contrast to other melons and fruits in fruit mixtures. Served alone, they are a nice change of pace from cantaloupe. (See also *Melon*.)

PERSIMMON — A fruit produced by a tree belonging to the *Diospyros* genus. Although extremely astringent when unripe, persimmons ripen to a delicious sweetness and juiciness. There are many different persimmon varieties, but two types are most prominent—the oriental persimmon and the American persimmon. The oriental or Japanese persimmon, the type most frequently marketed, is a tomatolike fruit with a reddish orange skin and a firmly attached green stem cap. The American or native persimmon is about the size of a plum, 1 to 1½ inches in diameter, and has yellow skin blushed with pink.

It is not known when oriental persimmons were first cultivated, but it has been fairly well established that this type of persimmon grew wild in southern China. Oriental persimmons were brought to Europe in the early 1800s, but they were not introduced to the United States until later. In the 1870s, United States Department of Agriculture plant explorers introduced a number of varieties suitable for cultivation. By the turn of the century, interest in persimmons had grown.

American persimmons have often been written about. Many of these early reports did not commend the fruit's flavor, possibly because the fruits had been eaten while still unripe. Captain John Smith, however, recognized their goodness when ripe by remarking that a persimmon is "as delicious as an apricock (apricot)." In any event, their usefulness grew to include persimmon breads, puddings, and salads.

How persimmons are produced: Both types of persimmons are grown worldwide. California is the main commercial producing area for oriental persimmons in the United States, although they are grown in other states in smaller quantities. American persimmons are not grown on a large scale.

Persimmon trees are propagated by budding and grafting the desired variety onto the seedlings or cuttings that are used for

When soft and bright-colored, persimmons are truly a winter delicacy. Serve halves or wedges with lime or lemon slices.

rootstocks. Both types can tolerate only minimal soil and climate changes. Oriental persimmon trees rarely grow over 40 feet tall and can be cultivated as far north as Virginia. American persimmon trees, on the other hand, can achieve 50 to 100 foot heights and will grow even in lower Michigan and western New York.

Nutritional value: Oriental and American persimmons differ as much in nutritive value as they do in appearance. Oriental persimmons are high in water and, thus, are low in calories. One 3½-ounce portion of oriental persimmon (1 medium) yields 80 calories. The same amount of American persimmon contains 130 calories.

In vitamin and mineral content, there is quite a difference between the two types. Oriental persimmons are considered fair sources of vitamin A, and they contain small amounts of the other vitamins and minerals. In American persimmons, vitamin A and the B vitamins are missing, but a lot of vitamin C is present.

How to select and store: American persimmons are usually available only in local areas of the South, but oriental persimmons are distributed nationwide from October to January. Resembling tomatoes in shape and firmness, these persimmons with stem caps attached should be firm, plump, and reddish orange.

Tannins present in underripe persimmons are responsible for the puckery taste associated with this fruit. Thus, most people agree that it is best to serve persimmons when they are fully ripe and full of sweet, rich flavor.

If the persimmons are not completely ripe at the time of purchase, they must be set in a cool, dark place and allowed to fully ripen. When ripe, refrigerate persimmons, handling them carefully, and use them within a day or two.

How to prepare and use: Persimmons may be peeled and sliced or cut in wedges. An unpeeled half may be served to be eaten out of the shell with a spoon. An accompaniment of lemon or lime slices is generally welcomed. Serve wedges with cream for breakfast. You can even add persimmon slices to grapefruit and avocado for a side dish salad. (See also *Fruit.*)

PESTO *(pe′ stō)*—An Italian sauce that is used with all kinds of pastas. Pesto contains basil plus garlic, olive oil, and grated cheese. (See also *Italian Cookery.*)

PETITE MARMITE *(puh tēt′ mär′ mīt)*—A classic French soup named for the marmite or earthenware pot in which the soup is prepared and served. The clear broth is made with beef or chicken marrow bones and vegetables. Sometimes, cabbage balls and pieces of meat are added. Slices of toasted French bread topped with grated cheese are typically used as garnish.

PETIT FOUR *(pet′ ē fōr′)*—Any small, individual cake, biscuit, cookie, or confection. The French words *petit* meaning small and *four* meaning oven allude to the first petits fours served to the French king Louis XIV and his court. These delicate cakes were served right from the oven.

The phrase now refers to a variety of sweets, the best known of which are the tiny pieces of cake coated with a fondant-like icing and intricately decorated.

Carry out a pink party theme with pastel-iced Petits Fours and scoops of pink ice cream drizzled with a rosy fruit sauce.

Petits Fours

Dainty tea cakes—

¼ cup butter or margarine
¼ cup shortening
1 cup sugar
½ teaspoon vanilla
¼ teaspoon almond extract
. . .
2 cups sifted cake flour
3 teaspoons baking powder
¼ teaspoon salt
¾ cup milk
¾ cup egg whites (6)
¼ cup sugar
Petits Fours Icing

Cream together butter and shortening. Gradually add 1 cup sugar, creaming till light. Stir in vanilla and almond extract. Sift together flour, baking powder, and salt. Add to creamed mixture alternately with milk, beating well after each addition. Beat egg whites till foamy; gradually add ¼ cup sugar, beating till soft peaks form. Fold into batter.

Turn into greased and lightly floured 13x9x2-inch pan. Bake at 350° about 40 minutes. Cool 10 minutes; remove from pan. Cool completely.

Cut cooled cake in 1½-inch diamonds, squares, or circles, using stiff paper pattern. Place cakes on rack with cookie sheet below. Spoon Petits Fours Icing over cakes. Let dry; add another coat of icing. Decorate with various garnishes: sliced almonds, snipped marshmallows, fruit slice flowers, or frosting flowers.

Petits Fours Icing: In covered 2-quart saucepan bring 3 cups granulated sugar, ¼ teaspoon cream of tartar, and 1½ cups hot water to boiling. Uncover; continue cooking to thin syrup (226°). Cool at room temperature (not over ice water) to lukewarm (110°). Stir in 1 teaspoon vanilla and sifted confectioners' sugar (about 2½ cups) till icing is of pouring consistency. Tint with desired food coloring.

PETITS POIS *(pet' e pwä')*—The French phrase for small, tender green peas. Although the phrase originally referred to a specific pea variety, it is now used to identify any small pea. (See also *Pea.*)

PETTICOAT TAIL—A buttery, bell-shaped Scottish shortbread so named because it looks like the petticoats worn by eighteenth-century English ladies.

PFEFFERNUSS *(fef' uh noōs, -uhr nûs)*—A traditional German Christmas cookie, spice-flavored and molded into balls the size of walnuts. The name (translated, it means peppernut) indicates the unusual spice which the cookie contains, black pepper. (See also *German Cookery.*)

Pfeffernuesse

In saucepan combine ¾ cup light molasses and ½ cup butter or margarine. Cook and stir till butter melts. Cool to room temperature.

Stir in 2 beaten eggs. Sift together 4¼ cups sifted all-purpose flour, ½ cup granulated sugar, 1¼ teaspoons baking soda, 1½ teaspoons ground cinnamon, ½ teaspoon ground cloves, ½ teaspoon ground nutmeg, and ⅛ teaspoon pepper. Add this mixture to the molasses mixture; mix well. Chill. Shape dough into 1-inch balls. Bake the cookies on a greased cookie sheet at 375° for about 12 minutes. Cool on rack; roll balls in confectioners' sugar. Makes about 4½ dozen cookies.

PHEASANT—A game bird prized as a culinary delicacy. Pheasant is related to the quail and partridge. Originally, the habitat of pheasants was limited to Asia where they were found in greatest numbers in India and Indo-China. In time, however, the wild bird was introduced into Europe and England, and late in the nineteenth century, British travelers took the bird to the United States. Today, pheasants abound throughout the northern United States and in southern Canada. In some locales, the pheasant even is considered the most important game-hunting bird.

Pheasants are easily recognizable. The typical male bird has bluish green feathers and a long tail. Because the tail of the male is so brilliantly colored in full plumage, it is frequently reproduced on canvas in still life compositions. In contrast, the feathers of the female bird are greatly subdued and the tail is quite short.

The flavor of pheasant is sometimes likened to that of poultry and venison. Tender and distinctive, the meat is considered a gourmet delicacy when properly aged after shooting and prepared carefully. The flavor of pheasant is best if the bird is allowed to hang unplucked for a few days, with the period of aging dependent upon the temperature. Hung by the neck, the pheasant is ready to cook when the tail feathers are easily removed. According to connoisseurs of pheasant, the flavor of the bird that is allowed to hang unplucked far surpasses that of the bird which was plucked before hanging.

For best eating quality, select a young pheasant. Youg birds have less fat than do the older birds, and their meat is quite tender. (Connoisseurs favor young hen pheasants, if available, because of the hens' tender meat.) To tenderize an older bird, first marinate the meat and then cook it with moist heat.

As with other game birds, the amount of fat covering the pheasant is relatively low. Consequently, the dressed bird is best if larded with a few bacon slices or some salt pork during roasting.

Generally, pheasants weigh from 2 to 5 pounds. The young bird is easily identified by its short, round claws and the pointed outer feather on its wing.

Although pheasants are frequently secured by the sportsman, the enjoyment of this wild game is not limited to the hunter. Fortunately, pheasants are available frozen in specialty meat markets. Popularly prepared by roasting, pheasant is also delicious when used in casseroles, meat pies, and aspics. (See also *Game*.)

How to roast pheasant

Young birds are best for roasting. Salt inside of one 1- to 3-pound ready-to-cook pheasant. Stuff as desired. Truss; place, breast side up, on rack in shallow roasting pan. Lay bacon slices over breast. Roast, uncovered, at 350° till tender, about 1 to 2½ hours. (Time will vary with age of bird.) Baste occasionally with drippings. To prevent excess browning, place foil loosely over top of bird. Allow 1 to 1½ pounds per serving.

Smothered Pheasant

¼ cup all-purpose flour
½ teaspoon salt
⅛ teaspoon pepper
1 1- to 3-pound ready-to-cook
   pheasant, cut up
½ cup shortening
2 medium onions, sliced
1 cup water, milk, *or* light cream
   Gravy

In plastic bag combine flour, salt, and pepper. Add pheasant pieces, a few at a time, making certain each piece is well coated. In Dutch oven brown pheasant slowly in hot shortening, turning once. Arrange onions atop pheasant; add water, milk, *or* light cream. Cover tightly; cook over low heat or bake at 325° till tender, about 1 hour. Remove pheasant, reserving pan drippings. Makes 2 to 4 servings.

Gravy: In screw-top jar shake ¾ cup milk with 3 tablespoons all-purpose flour, 1 teaspoon salt, and dash pepper till blended. Stir into 3 tablespoons reserved pan drippings in skillet. Add ¾ cup milk. Cook and stir till thick and bubbly. Cook and stir 2 to 3 minutes more. Pass with pheasant. Makes 1½ cups.

Roast Sherried Pheasant

1 1½- to 3-pound ready-to-cook
 pheasant
Salt
1 small bay leaf
1 clove garlic
 Few celery leaves
1 slice lemon
3 to 4 slices bacon
 Hot cooked rice
 Sherry Sauce

Season inside of pheasant with salt. Stuff with bay leaf, garlic, celery leaves, and lemon slice. Cover breast with bacon slices; truss. Follow directions for roasting pheasant. Remove pheasant from the roasting pan, reserving drippings in the pan. Remove string and discard the stuffing mixture. Serve the pheasant on a bed of hot cooked rice. Accompany with Sherry Sauce. Makes 2 or 3 servings.

Sherry Sauce: Blend together 1 cup chicken broth with 2 tablespoons all-purpose flour; add to reserved drippings in roasting pan. Stir over moderate heat, scraping loose the browned drippings. Cook, stirring constantly, till mixture is thickened and bubbly. Stir in 3 tablespoons dry sherry. Pass sauce with pheasant.

Pheasant with Wild Rice

⅓ cup uncooked wild rice, rinsed
2 tablespoons butter or margarine,
 softened
¼ cup light raisins
½ teaspoon ground sage
⅛ teaspoon salt

· · ·

1 1½- to 3-pound ready-to-cook
 pheasant
Salt
3 to 4 slices bacon

In saucepan cook wild rice in boiling, salted water till tender, according to package directions; drain. Stir in softened butter or margarine, raisins, sage, and ⅛ teaspoon salt.

Season the inside of the pheasant with salt. Stuff the bird with wild rice stuffing; truss. Place bacon slices over breast of pheasant. Follow directions given in box for roasting pheasant. Makes 2 or 3 servings.

Pheasant in Wine Sauce

¼ cup all-purpose flour
1½ teaspoons paprika
½ teaspoon salt
⅛ teaspoon pepper
1 1½- to 3-pound ready-to-cook
 pheasant, quartered
2 tablespoons shortening
1 3-ounce can broiled sliced
 mushrooms, undrained
½ cup dry sauterne
¼ cup sliced green onion

In plastic bag combine flour, paprika, salt, and pepper. Add 2 or 3 pheasant pieces at a time and shake. In skillet brown pheasant on all sides in hot shortening. Add undrained mushrooms, sauterne, and onion. Cover and simmer till tender, about 1 hour. Serves 2 or 3.

PHOSPHATE BAKING POWDER — A type of baking powder containing calcium or sodium phosphate as the acid salt. A single-action leavener, phosphate baking powder releases carbon dioxide when combined with a liquid. (See also *Baking Powder.*)

PHOSPHORUS — A mineral required by the body to carry out its normal metabolic processes, to aid in the development of bones and teeth, to maintain normal blood chemistry, to transport fatty acids, and to conduct nerve impulses. Widely distributed in foods, phosphorus is found in liver, lean meat, fish, poultry, eggs, milk, cheese, legumes, leafy vegetables, nuts, and whole grains. (See also *Nutrition.*)

PHYLLO — Another spelling for the Greek pastry called fillo. Phyllo is used in desserts and appetizers. (See also *Fillo.*)

PICADILLO — A Spanish hash prepared with ground veal and ground pork. Other ingredients in picadillo include tomatoes, onions, garlic, olives, raisins, and almonds.

PICCALILLI *(pik′ uh lil′ ē)* — A highly seasoned relish that originated in East India. Piccalilli is made with green tomatoes, green and red peppers, cabbage, cucumbers, onions, sugar, vinegar, and spices.

PICKEREL *(pik' uhr uhl, pik' ruhl)*—**1.** A small species of the pike family. **2.** The young fish of the larger species in the pike family. A lean fish found in fresh-water lakes, it measures about 12 inches in length. Pickerel is available whole, dressed, or filleted. (See also *Pike*.)

PICKLE—**1.** A preservation method whereby vegetables or fruits are canned in a brine or vinegar. **2.** The name for a vegetable or fruit canned in a brine or vinegar.

The popularity of pickling dates back to colonial days. In an attempt to stabilize the food supply from the more abundant to the lean years, the early-day housewife employed many methods of preserving foods. Among these methods was pickling. However, pickling was not limited to the colonial kitchen. The pickle barrel was a mainstay in every country store. For a small price, the customer had his choice of a wide variety of pickles. Today, the numerous types of pickles found in the supermarkets indicate their popularity, just as home-canned pickles remain a source of pride for many homemakers.

Vegetable pickles are frequently made from cucumbers or green tomatoes, although other vegetables are used, too. Sometimes sweet, sometimes sour, the pickling liquid may or may not contain spices. During pickling, cucumbers, green beans, and green tomatoes change from a bright green to an olive green color.

Fruit pickles are commonly prepared from crab apples, peaches, pears, figs, and watermelon rind. Most often sweet in flavor, pickled fruits are frequently spiced. They are made from small whole fruits or uniform pieces of fruit. When properly pickled, they retain their natural color and have a firm texture without being watery.

How to prepare: Vegetable pickles are usually packed cold in jars and covered with a boiling liquid. They are then processed in a water bath canner according to recipe directions. Occasionally, vegetables are cured in a brine for several weeks before they are canned. However, this method is not recommended in the home since it is difficult to maintain a constant temperature and brine strength.

Pickle pointers

• Select fresh, firm fruits and vegetables for pickling. Fruit is best if slightly underripe.
• Use unwaxed cucumbers for pickling and remove all blossoms. For best results, pickle cucumbers within 24 hours after picking.
• Salt is used for flavor and to help crisp pickles. Use pure granulated pickling salt or *uniodized* table salt. Avoid using iodized table salt, as it tends to cloud the brine.
• Choose a high-grade cider vinegar for pickling unless a light-colored pickle is desired. Then use a white vinegar. Acidity of vinegar should be 4 to 6 percent (40 to 60 grain).
• Use fresh herbs and spices when pickling. Wrap seasonings in a cheesecloth for easy removal at the end of the cooking process.
• Unless brown sugar is specified in a recipe, use granulated sugar. Brown sugar produces a change in color and flavor in pickles.
• Use soft water for preparing the brine. If water is naturally hard, boil for 15 minutes, then let stand 24 hours. Carefully remove scum from top of water and dip water from kettle so as not to disturb the sediment in the bottom. Add 1 tablespoon vinegar per gallon of boiling water before using in pickle brine.
• Use utensils made of enameled ware, aluminum, glass, stainless steel, or stoneware.
• Shriveled pickles are produced by using too strong a salt, sugar, or vinegar solution; overcooking; or overprocessing.
• Soft pickles are the result of using too little salt or acid, insufficient processing, or poor sealing of the product.

Unlike vegetable pickles, fruit pickles are generally canned using a hot pack. The fruit is cooked in a syrup until almost tender and then processed in a water bath canner. Some people believe that the fruit has an improved flavor and is more plump if allowed to stand in the syrup several hours after cooking.

As with all types of canning, top-quality ingredients are necessary to obtain satisfactory results. If pickled whole, use those that are medium to small in size. To pickle fruits and vegetables, use the following detailed directions.

Sweet and spicy homemade Watermelon Pickles lend a refreshing accent to a full-course dinner or to a quick lunch.

1. Check jars and lids for flaws. Discard any with chips or cracks. Use new metal sealing disks or rubbers.

2. Wash jars in hot, sudsy water; rinse. Wash lids according to manufacturer's directions. Place jars in hot water till ready to use. They needn't be sterilized, as this is done during processing.

3. Place water bath canner on heat with enough water to cover tops of jars.

4. Prepare pickles according to recipe directions on the following pages.

5. Fill hot jars firmly, but be sure the liquid fills in around the fruit or vegetable. Leave ½-inch headspace between the food-liquid mixture and top of jar. Force out air bubbles from filled jars by carefully working blade of table knife down sides of jars. Add more liquid if needed, but keep the original ½-inch headspace.

6. Adjust jar caps: (**a**) for *two-piece metal lids,* wipe sealing edge of jar with clean cloth to remove food particles. Put metal lid on jar with sealing compound next to glass. Screw band tight. (**b**) For *porcelain-lined, zinc screw covers,* fit wet rubber ring on jar; wipe jar rim and ring with clean cloth. Partially seal jar by screwing the zinc cover down firmly. Then turn the cover back ¼ inch.

7. Lower jars in rack into water bath canner (have water hot or just below boiling point). Be sure jars do not touch. Cover the canner. The processing time begins when the water returns to a rolling boil. Boil gently during entire processing time. Add more *boiling* water as needed to keep jars covered. Process pickles, using times indicated in recipes. Note altitude corrections (see page 391).

8. After processing, remove hot jars from canner. Complete seal if using zinc covers. Cool on rack or cloth, a few inches apart, and away from drafts for time specified by lid manufacturer.

9. Check seals on jars when cold. To test jar with metal lid, press center of lid; if lid is drawn down, jar is sealed. For other types of covers, tip jar to check for leakage. If jar isn't sealed, use immediately; or check jar for flaws and reprocess with a new lid.

10. To store cooled, filled jars, remove screw bands from two-piece metal lids. Wipe jars; label with contents and date. Store in a cool, dry, dark place.

To open, puncture metal disk; lift up. For zinc screw covers, pull out rubber ring before unscrewing cap. Look for spoilage —leaks, bulging lids, or off-odor. Never taste with these signs; discard.

How to use: Regardless of whether pickles are canned commercially or in the home, they provide a welcome accent in the menu. Their sweet, tart, and/or spicy flavor lends a sharp contrast to other foods.

Pickles are a natural for serving on a relish plate with an assortment of crisp vegetables. Likewise, chopped cucumber pickles add zest to sandwich fillings, dips, spreads, salads, meat loaves, and casseroles. For many pickle enthusiasts, no sandwich or hamburger is complete without a layering of sweet or dill pickles.

Fruit pickles are particularly appealing when used as a garnish or served as a meat accompaniment. For special occasions, arrange bright and colorful pickled peaches or crab apples alongside the meat entrée. (See also *Canning.*)

Home-canned Dill Pickles add a special note to the familiar assortment of relishes offered either before or during the meal.

Dill Pickles

A favorite you'll always want to keep on hand—

Scrub 3- or 4-inch cucumbers with brush. Pack loosely in hot quart jars. To *each quart* add: 3 or 4 heads fresh dill and 1 teaspoon mustard seed. Make brine for *each quart* by combining 2 cups water, 1 cup vinegar, and 1 tablespoon granulated pickling salt; bring to boiling.

Fill hot jars to within ½ inch of top with brine. Adjust lids. Process in boiling water bath for 20 minutes (see page 1657, step 7).

Sweet-Sour Pickles

Wash 3½ pounds 2½-inch cucumbers (about 50). Dissolve ½ cup granulated pickling salt in 4 cups boiling water; pour over cucumbers. Let stand in liquid till cool; drain.

Combine 1½ quarts cider vinegar, 2 cups water, 1 tablespoon mixed pickling spice, and 3 cups sugar; bring to boiling. Pour mixture over cucumbers; let stand for 24 hours. Bring cucumbers and syrup to boiling; pack in hot jars to within ½ inch of jar top. Adjust lids. Process in boiling water bath for 5 minutes (see page 1657, step 7). Makes 5 pints.

Mustard Pickles

>   1 large head cauliflower
>   1 quart small green tomatoes, cut in wedges
>   3 green peppers, cut in strips
> 1½ pounds 2-inch cucumbers, halved lengthwise
>   3 cups pickling onions, peeled
>   1 cup granulated pickling salt
>   4 cups water
>   2 cups sugar
>   1 cup all-purpose flour
>   ½ cup dry mustard
>   1 tablespoon turmeric
>   5 cups cider vinegar
>   5 cups water

Break cauliflower into flowerets. Combine first 5 ingredients. Cover with pickling salt and 4 cups water; let stand in cool place overnight.

Drain; cover with boiling water. Let stand 10 minutes; drain. Combine sugar and remaining ingredients; cook and stir till thickened and bubbly. Add vegetables; cook till tender.

Fill hot jars to within ½ inch of top; adjust lids. Process in boiling water bath for 5 minutes (see page 1657, step 7). Makes 10 pints.

Watermelon Pickles

>   2 pounds watermelon rind
>   ¼ cup granulated pickling salt
>   2 cups sugar
>   1 cup white vinegar
>   1 tablespoon broken stick cinnamon
> 1½ teaspoons whole cloves
>   ½ lemon, thinly sliced
>   5 maraschino cherries, halved (optional)

Trim dark green and pink from rind; cut in 1-inch cubes. Measure 7 cups. Soak overnight in solution of salt and 1 quart water (add more, if needed, to cover). Drain; rinse rind. Cover with cold water. Cook till just tender; drain.

Combine sugar, vinegar, 1 cup water, and spices. Simmer 10 minutes; strain. Add rind, lemon, and cherries. Simmer till rind is clear; pack in hot jars to ½ inch from top. Adjust lids; process in boiling water bath for 5 minutes (see page 1657, step 7). Makes 2½ pints.

Sweet Pickles

Select 9½ pounds of 3- to 4-inch cucumbers (about 150). Wash and cover cucumbers with hot salt brine made of 1 cup granulated pickling salt to each 2 quarts water. Cool; cover with large plate or lid with weight atop to keep cucumbers in brine. Let stand for 7 days.

Drain; cover with hot water. Let stand 24 hours. Drain; cover again with hot water. Let stand 24 hours. Drain; split cucumbers.

Combine 12 cups sugar, 8 cups cider vinegar, 1½ teaspoons celery seed, 8 sticks stick cinnamon, and 1 cup prepared horseradish. Bring to boiling; pour mixture over cucumbers. Cool; cover. Let stand overnight. Drain syrup from cucumbers each morning for 4 days; reheat syrup and pour over cucumbers. Each time, let cucumbers cool in syrup before covering.

On the fifth day, remove cinnamon sticks and bring cucumbers in syrup to boiling. Pack cucumbers and syrup into hot jars to within ½ inch of jar top. Adjust lids. Process cucumbers in boiling water bath for 5 minutes (see page 1657, step 7). Makes about 13 pints.

Crisp Pickle Slices

The popular bread-and-butter type—

> 4 quarts sliced, unpeeled, medium cucumbers
> 6 medium white onions, sliced (6 cups)
> 2 green peppers, sliced (1⅔ cups)
> 3 cloves garlic
> ⅓ cup granulated pickling salt
> 5 cups sugar
> 3 cups cider vinegar
> 1½ teaspoons turmeric
> 1½ teaspoons celery seed
> 2 tablespoons mustard seed

Combine cucumber, onion, green pepper, and whole garlic cloves. Add salt; cover with cracked ice. Mix thoroughly. Let stand for 3 hours; drain well. Remove garlic. Combine sugar and remaining ingredients; pour over cucumber mixture. Bring to boiling. Pack cucumber mixture into hot jars to ½ inch from top; adjust lids. Process in boiling water bath for 5 minutes (see page 1657, step 7). Makes 8 pints.

Mixed Pickles are a colorful combination of fresh garden vegetables, including red and green peppers, cucumbers, and carrots.

Mixed Pickles

> 4 medium cucumbers
> Granulated pickling salt
> • • •
> 2 medium carrots
> 2 medium green peppers
> 2 medium red peppers
> • • •
> 2 cups sugar
> 1½ cups vinegar
> 1 tablespoon celery seed
> 1 tablespoon mustard seed
> 1 teaspoon salt
> ½ teaspoon turmeric

Wash cucumbers; do not peel. Cut into sticks 2x½ inches, to measure 7 cups. Place cucumber sticks in large glass or earthenware bowl; cover with brine made of ½ cup granulated pickling salt to *each* quart of water. Let cucumbers stand overnight; drain and rinse.

Cut carrots and peppers in sticks ½ inch wide. Cook carrots in small amount of boiling, salted water for 5 minutes; drain. In saucepan combine sugar and next 5 ingredients; cook and stir till sugar is dissolved. Add cucumbers, carrots, and peppers; heat to boiling. Pack in hot, sterilized jars and seal. Makes 4 pints.

Pickled Dilled Beans

Excellent way to use up a bumper crop—

>   2 pounds green beans
>   Boiling water
>   • • •
>   1 cup white vinegar
>   3 cups water
>   2 tablespoons pickling salt
>   2 teaspoons dillweed
> ¼ teaspoon cayenne
>   2 cloves garlic, crushed

Wash beans; drain. Trim ends. Cut beans to fit jars. Cover beans with boiling water; cook 3 minutes. Drain. Pack lengthwise into hot jars, leaving ½-inch headspace. In saucepan or Dutch oven combine vinegar, 3 cups water, pickling salt, dillweed, cayenne, and garlic; bring to boiling. Cover beans with pickling liquid, leaving ½-inch headspace. Adjust lids. Process in boiling water bath (pints and quarts) 10 minutes. Makes 4 pints.

Pickled Mushrooms and Onions

Use these pickles for a delicious, interesting relish tray or appetizer at your next party—

>   1 pound fresh whole mushrooms
>   • • •
>   2 medium onions, thinly sliced and
>   separated into rings (1 cup)
> 1½ cups red wine vinegar
> 1½ cups water
> ½ cup packed brown sugar
>   4 teaspoons pickling salt
>   1 teaspoon dried tarragon, crushed

Thoroughly wash the mushrooms; trim stems. In 3-quart saucepan combine onion rings, red wine vinegar, water, brown sugar, pickling salt, and the tarragon; bring the mixture to boiling. Add the mushrooms; simmer, uncovered, 5 minutes. Lift the mushrooms and onion rings from the pickling liquid with slotted spoon. Reserve the liquid; keep hot.

Pack the vegetables in hot jars, leaving ½-inch headspace. Cover with boiling pickling liquid, leaving ½-inch headspace. Adjust lids. Process in boiling water bath (half-pints and pints) 5 minutes. Makes 4 half-pints.

Pickled Sweet Red Peppers

Make several extra jars of these bright peppers to give as gifts next Christmas—

> 2½ pounds sweet red peppers
>   Boiling water
>   • • •
>   2 cups sugar
>   2 cups tarragon vinegar
>   2 cups water
> ½ teaspoon celery seed
> ½ teaspoon mustard seed
>   2 cloves garlic, crushed
>   1 teaspoon salt

Thoroughly wash the sweet red peppers. Remove tops and seeds from the peppers. Cut peppers in quarters or sixths lengthwise, or in strips. In medium saucepan cook red peppers 3 minutes in boiling water. Drain peppers. In 6- to 8-quart kettle or Dutch oven combine sugar, tarragon vinegar, 2 cups water, celery seed, mustard seed, crushed garlic, and salt.

Bring the mixture to boiling; simmer 5 minutes. Pack hot peppers into hot wide-mouth jars, leaving ½-inch headspace. Cover with boiling pickling liquid, leaving ½-inch headspace. Adjust lids. Process in boiling water bath (pints) 10 minutes. Makes 4 pints.

Pickled Onions

Perfect flavor complement to broiled steak—

> 1½ pounds pearl onions
>   2 cups water
>   2 tablespoons pickling salt
> 1½ cups white vinegar
> ⅓ cup sugar
>   1 teaspoon mixed pickling spices

Drop onions in boiling water to cover; boil 3 minutes. Drain; place in cold water. Cut root end; squeeze stem end to remove onion skin. Combine 2 cups water and pickling salt; pour over onions. Let stand 12 hours. Drain; rinse thoroughly. Combine vinegar, sugar, and pickling spices; bring to boiling. Pack onions into hot jars, leaving ½-inch headspace. Cover with pickling liquid, leaving ½-inch headspace. Adjust lids. Process in boiling water bath (half-pints) 10 minutes. Makes 4 half-pints.

Pickled Beets

Use either small whole beets or cubed large ones—

>   3 pounds small whole beets*
>   Boiling water
>   · · ·
>   2 cups vinegar
>   1 cup water
>   ½ cup sugar
>   1 teaspoon whole allspice
>   6 whole cloves
>   3 inches stick cinnamon

Wash beets, leaving on root and 1 inch of tops. Cover beets with boiling water; simmer 25 minutes. Drain. Slip off skins and trim beets. In large kettle combine vinegar, 1 cup water, and sugar. Tie allspice, cloves, and stick cinnamon in cheesecloth bag. Add spice bag to pickling liquid. Bring to boiling; simmer 15 minutes. Pack beets into hot jars, leaving ½-inch headspace. Cover beets with boiling pickling liquid, leaving ½-inch headspace. Adjust lids. Process in boiling water bath (half-pints) 30 minutes. Makes 3 half-pints.

*For large beets, wash, remove tops, and cook as directed. Slip off skins; cube.

Green Tomato Dill Pickles

Salvage green tomatoes from the vine when frost comes by picking them and making these pickles—

>   5 pounds small firm green tomatoes
>   Fresh dill heads *or* dillseed
>   Garlic cloves
>   Whole cloves
>   · · ·
>   4 cups vinegar
>   ⅓ cup salt
>   4 cups water

Wash green tomatoes; slice ¼ inch thick. Pack tomatoes loosely into hot quart jars, leaving ½-inch headspace. To each quart add 3 or 4 heads fresh dill or 2 tablespoons dillseed, 1 clove garlic, and 1 whole clove. In saucepan combine vinegar, salt, and 4 cups water. Bring to boiling. Pour boiling pickling liquid over tomatoes, leaving ½-inch headspace. Adjust lids. Process in boiling water bath (quarts) 20 minutes. Makes 5 quarts.

Pickled Artichoke Hearts

Gourmets will love this recipe—

>   4 pounds small artichokes
>   4 cups white vinegar
>   4 quarts water
>   · · ·
>   4 cups water
>   1 cup white wine vinegar
>   1 clove garlic, crushed
>   1 tablespoon salt

Wash artichokes. Cut off stem and ½ inch from top. Pull off coarser outer leaves. In 8- to 10-quart kettle or Dutch oven bring 4 cups white vinegar and 4 quarts water to boiling; add artichokes. Cover; simmer till leaf pulls off easily, about 10 minutes. Drain.

Cut artichokes in half; remove choke. Combine 4 cups water, wine vinegar, garlic, and salt to make brine. Bring to boiling. Pack artichoke hearts into hot jars, leaving ½-inch headspace. Pour boiling hot brine over artichokes, leaving ½-inch headspace; seal. Adjust lids. Process in boiling water bath (pints) 15 minutes. Makes 6 pints pickled artichoke hearts.

Sweet Pickled Carrots

If you want to try canning during the winter, just use carrots from the supermarket—

>   6 pounds medium carrots (about 36)
>   · · ·
>   3 cups sugar
>   3 cups vinegar
>   3 cups water
>   ⅓ cup mustard seed
>   6 inches stick cinnamon
>   6 whole cloves

Peel carrots. Cut carrots lengthwise into quarters. Cook the carrots in boiling, salted water just till tender, 7 to 8 minutes; drain. In 8- to 10-quart kettle or Dutch oven combine sugar, vinegar, water, mustard seed, stick cinnamon, and whole cloves.

Bring to boiling; simmer 20 minutes. Pack carrots into hot jars, leaving ½-inch headspace. Cover with vinegar mixture, leaving ½-inch headspace. Adjust lids. Process in boiling water bath (pints) 5 minutes. Makes 6 pints.

PICKLING SPICE—A blend of several whole spices commonly used for pickling. Although the blend varies somewhat, mixed pickling spice generally includes the following whole spices: allspice, black and white peppercorns, bay leaves, cardamom, cassia, chilies, cloves, dillseed, fennel seed, ginger, mace, and mustard seed. Larger, whole spices are broken into smaller pieces before they are added.

Most frequently used for making pickles and preserving meat, mixed pickling spice is well-suited for use in long-cooking dishes. It is excellent as a seasoning for stews, pot roasts, soups, marinades, shrimp, boiled tongue, beets, and cabbage. To use, wrap spices in a cheesecloth bag for easy removal. (See also *Spice*.)

PICNIC—A meal generally served out of doors. It may be as simple as a loaf of crusty bread, a chunk of cheese, and a bottle of wine popularly eaten as a picnic lunch by tourists motoring through Europe. Or it may be a meal served in courses from the tailgate of a station wagon before a football game. How pleasurable the picnic is depends not only on good company and good weather, but also on good planning before the picnic.

For a spur-of-the-moment picnic, pack assorted sandwich ingredients for on-the-spot assembly, crisp relishes, fresh fruit, and beverages into the picnic basket. For a well-chilled beverage that is just right for drinking when you arrive at your eating spot, keep individual serving-sized cans of fruit or vegetable juice in the freezer.

When sandwiches are made with lettuce and tomato slices, pack vegetables separately to keep them cool and crisp; add to sandwiches just before eating. Likewise, keep meats, salads, and relishes cooled in insulated bags or pack them in a portable ice chest. Use vacuum containers to keep foods either steaming hot or well chilled. Don't try to tote and serve jellied foods if the picnic is further away than your porch or patio. Pack dressings separately and toss with salads at picnic time.

Take advantage of paper and plastic plates, bowls, cups, and utensils. Light in weight and easy to pack, disposable items are a blessing at cleanup time.

Cheesy Corned Beef Sandwiches

1 12-ounce can corned beef, broken in small pieces
4 ounces sharp process American cheese, diced (1 cup)
½ cup mayonnaise
2 tablespoons sweet pickle relish
1 tablespoon instant minced onion
8 onion rolls or hamburger buns, split and buttered

Toss together first 5 ingredients; spoon into buns. Wrap in heavy foil. Heat over *medium* coals 12 to 15 minutes; turn often. Serves 8.

Ham with Crab Apple Glaze

1 27-ounce jar spiced whole crab apples
1 cup brown sugar
1 fully cooked, center-cut ham slice, about 1 inch thick (about 1½ pounds)

At home before the picnic, drain spiced crab apples, reserving ½ cup syrup. In small saucepan combine reserved syrup and brown sugar; heat and stir till mixture is boiling. Remove from heat; cool. Pour mixture into crab apple jar or other container for transporting to picnic site. Wrap crab apples in foil; seal.

At picnic site, open foil-wrapped crab apples and drizzle a little of the syrup mixture over apples; reseal foil and place apples at edge of grill till heated through.

Meanwhile, grill ham over *low* coals for 10 to 15 minutes on each side. Brush grilled ham with syrup mixture; cook 1 to 2 minutes. Turn; brush second side of ham with syrup mixture and cook 1 to 2 minutes more. Pass warm crab apples with ham. Makes 6 servings.

Onion Potatoes

Scrub 6 medium baking potatoes; cut each crosswise into ½-inch slices. Blend ½ cup softened butter with 1 envelope dry onion soup mix; spread on one side of each potato slice. Reassemble potatoes; wrap each in foil and seal. Bake on grill over coals till done, about 45 minutes to 1 hour; turn once. Serves 6.

PICNIC SHOULDER—1. A wholesale cut from the side of the pork that includes the arm and shank sections of the shoulder. **2.** The name of a retail cut taken from the wholesale cut of the same name.

The wholesale picnic shoulder is marketed fresh, cured (pickled), or cured and smoked. Roasts cut from this portion include picnic shoulder, rolled picnic shoulder, and cushion picnic shoulder. They are cooked to an internal temperature of 170° F. either by roasting or cooking in liquid. Other retail cuts which come from the wholesale picnic shoulder are arm steaks and pork hocks. (See also *Pork*.)

Italian Picnic Shoulder

Boldly flavored with garlic and vinegar—

   1 5- to 6-pound smoked picnic
      shoulder
   6 garlic cloves, quartered
   ¾ cup vinegar

Remove skin from smoked picnic shoulder. Place picnic in 10-quart Dutch oven; cover with water. Add garlic and vinegar to meat. Cover; simmer for 2½ to 3 hours. Remove from liquid; place roast in shallow pan. Bake at 350° for 15 to 20 minutes. Makes 8 to 12 servings.

Grill specialties, such as Ham with Crab Apple Glaze and Onion Potatoes, are partially prepared at home, then cooked at the picnic site. Complete menu with a salad and bread.

Smoked Pork Dinner

    1 3- to 4-pound cook-before-eating
        smoked picnic shoulder
    1 medium onion, chopped (½ cup)
    ½ cup chopped celery
    ¼ teaspoon garlic powder
    1 bay leaf
    6 medium potatoes, peeled and halved
    6 medium carrots, peeled and halved
    2 10-ounce packages frozen Brussels
        sprouts

Place smoked picnic shoulder in Dutch oven; cover with water. Add onion, celery, garlic powder, and bay leaf. Cover; bring to boiling. Reduce heat; simmer till almost tender, 2½ to 3 hours. Add potatoes and carrots; cover and simmer for about 15 minutes. Add Brussels sprouts; simmer 15 to 20 minutes longer. Discard the bay leaf. Makes 9 to 12 servings.

Pork and Potato Supper

    6 pork arm steaks (about 2½ pounds)
    ¼ cup all-purpose flour
    1 teaspoon salt
        Dash pepper
    1 10½-ounce can condensed chicken
        broth
    4 medium potatoes, peeled and sliced
        ½ inch thick (4 cups)
    2 medium onions, thinly sliced
        Salt
        Pepper
    2 tablespoons snipped parsley
        Paprika

Trim the excess fat from pork steaks. In a large skillet heat the trimmings till about 2 tablespoons fat accumulate; discard the trimmings. Combine all-purpose flour, 1 teaspoon salt, and dash pepper; coat arm steaks with flour mixture. In skillet brown steaks on both sides in hot fat, about 10 to 15 minutes. Drain off any excess fat.

Add condensed chicken broth. Cover tightly and simmer till steaks are almost tender, about 25 to 30 minutes. Place potato and onion slices over meat; season with salt and pepper. Cover and simmer till potatoes are tender, about 25 to 30 minutes longer. Sprinkle with snipped parsley and paprika. Makes 6 servings.

Dressed-Up Pork Steaks

    4 pork arm or blade steaks
        (about 2 pounds)
        Salt
        Pepper
    1 egg
    2½ cups soft bread crumbs
    ½ cup finely chopped celery
    ¼ cup finely chopped onion
    1 teaspoon grated orange peel
        (optional)
    ½ cup orange juice
    ½ teaspoon ground sage
    ¼ teaspoon salt

Trim excess fat from steaks. In skillet heat trimmings till 2 tablespoons fat accumulate; discard trimmings. Brown steaks on both sides in hot fat; pour off excess fat. Season steaks with salt and pepper.

Beat egg. Add remaining ingredients; toss together lightly. Mound dressing atop steaks. Place steaks in skillet; pour ½ cup water over. Cover; simmer for 30 minutes. Uncover; simmer 5 minutes longer. Makes 4 servings.

Orange Pork Steaks

    6 pork arm or blade steaks
        (about 2½ pounds)
    4 medium sweet potatoes, peeled and
        cut in ½-inch-thick slices
    2 medium oranges
    ½ cup brown sugar
    ⅛ teaspoon salt
        Dash ground cinnamon
        Dash ground nutmeg
        Parsley (optional)

Trim excess fat from steaks. In skillet cook trimmings till 1 tablespoon fat accumulates; discard trimmings. Cook steaks slowly just till browned; sprinkle with salt. In a 13½x8¾x 1¾-inch baking dish arrange sweet potatoes. Slice one of the oranges thinly; place atop potatoes. Cover with steaks. Squeeze remaining orange; add water to juice to measure ½ cup. Combine orange juice, brown sugar, ⅛ teaspoon salt, and spices. Pour over steaks. Bake, covered, at 350° for 45 minutes. Uncover; bake 30 minutes more. Garnish with parsley, if desired. Makes 6 servings.